Getting Started
in TENNIS

BY PAUL METZLER

Getting Started in
Tennis

STERLING
PUBLISHING CO., INC. NEW YORK
Oak Tree Press Co., Ltd.
LONDON AND SYDNEY

BY THE SAME AUTHOR

Advanced Tennis

Athletic Institute Series

Baseball

Basketball

Girls' Basketball

Girls' Gymnastics

Gymnastics

Table Tennis

Tumbling and Trampolining

Wrestling

Third Printing, 1972

Copyright © 1972 by Paul Metzler
Published by Sterling Publishing Co., Inc.
419 Park Avenue South, New York, N.Y. 10016
British edition published by Oak Tree Press Co., Ltd., Nassau, Bahamas
Distributed in Australia by Oak Tree Press Co., Ltd.,
P.O. Box 34, Brickfield Hill, Sydney 2000, N.S.W.
Distributed in the United Kingdom and elsewhere in the British Commonwealth
by Ward Lock Ltd., 116 Baker Street, London W 1
Manufactured in the United States of America
All rights reserved
Library of Congress Catalog Card No.: 70-180467
ISBN 0–8069– 4050 –6   UK 7061 2355 7
4051 –4

CONTENTS

EVONNE GOOLAGONG, young Australian sensation, to whom this book is dedicated.

INTRODUCTION

YOU HAVE PLAYED a little tennis, watched it being played, and now you want to improve your game—or you would not have picked up this book. You know in general how the strokes are played, the purpose of the game, and how to score.

You have heard "spin" mentioned a lot and now you want to know the facts about it. You have probably seen a star crashing down aces and you want to know how you can serve something like that. You have realized that ball control must be the essence of the game and you would like to have the secret of it.

In the pages that follow you will be introduced to all these subjects—and many more—and given point-by-point explanations. If you can get a coach to help you learn your strokes, do so. This book is in line with modern coaching methods and will help you to grasp more quickly whatever your coach shows you. In case you cannot go to a coach or cannot afford one, this book shows you repeatedly what to look for in the strokes of experienced players, so that you may be your own coach. *It is important that you start your tennis correctly*, so that your later development will not be restricted in any way.

Follow the text and the drawings and you will almost certainly perform well on the court: Tennis is in the mind as much as in the arm. After reading this book, I think you will watch the champions with new eyes.

The book is uncomplicated. As you continue to practice, play, watch and learn, you will need information on the finer points of the game. These fine points, and much more about mental aspects, are set out in my book called *Advanced Tennis*. When your game progresses to that stage—rapidly, I hope—it will be waiting for you. This present book leads to it.

PAUL METZLER

1. ATTITUDE

BE INTERESTED in your strokes. This will make you want to play all the time, instead of only when the weather is perfect.

Never mind wind, heat or cold—be satisfied if it is not raining. Playing tennis under varying conditions will give you good practice in ball control and stroke-making.

If you are in your teens, you are fit enough to play all day long. Do not be discouraged if some infant beats you because he has been playing for several years. You have not made a late start. Your game at, say, 15 will be about the same whether you started at the age of 12 or 6.

No one of any age should decide he has a poor temperament for the game and that tennis is not for him. There is no need to feel shaky if you badly want to win. For it is only inexperience that causes you to worry about the result of a set or match *while* you are playing it. You soon learn to play for each point, one at a time, and even for each stroke during a point or rally. You will come to the stage when you can enjoy, perhaps grimly, the tightest match. Good strokes will give you a good match-temperament.

Your attitude towards your opponent can be much more lenient than you may have thought. You are not confined to being fiercely competitive and having a killer instinct. Everyone is different. Many people find they play better and win more when they don't go in for disliking their opponents. Others say they can't begin to understand this. Please yourself, and you won't be wrong.

On this tack, let's dispose of the only distasteful part of the whole game here and now. Some players cheat. You need to know how to look after yourself in such cases. Don't cheat in return. You may get a point or two back by return-cheating, but, aside from everything else, it is not the best way to win. Cheated calls are nearly all made on balls close to the line, so let this make you determined to hit your next shots well in. You may deservedly hate your opponent, but my point is that this concentration on playing-the-ball-in will improve your play and is more likely to make you a winner than anything else you can do. It is easier said than done, but do it.

Perhaps you are surprised at my saying this. However, this is what match-toughened players do. You will probably receive a few more surprises in this book, but they will not be surprises to good match-players or coaches.

If you have cheated now and then yourself, cut it out. Whenever you meet an opponent who knows his tennis and intensifies his concentration, you will lose by attempting unfair play. And on the way you will earn yourself some dreadful contempt and humiliation, sooner or later. When you play a sport, *be* a sport.

If you have an umpire, unless he makes an obvious mistake that your opponent recognizes as clearly as you do, play to his calls. Don't complain about close calls against you and don't deliberately lose the next point if a close call was wrongly given to your advantage.This sort of thing makes the umpire look foolish and feel uncertain, and if you and your opponent continue to do it, it will ruin the whole set.

You have heard about "brains." Some players are said to use their heads. Others, although perhaps normally clever, are said to have left their brains behind them in the dressing-room. "Brains" is a misleading term. It really means knowing the game. You will know it if you understand this book and apply it to suit your own game.

We will not prolong Attitude. It could become involved and keep us away from the court. We will take it as it comes, throughout the book.

We want to get on to ball control.

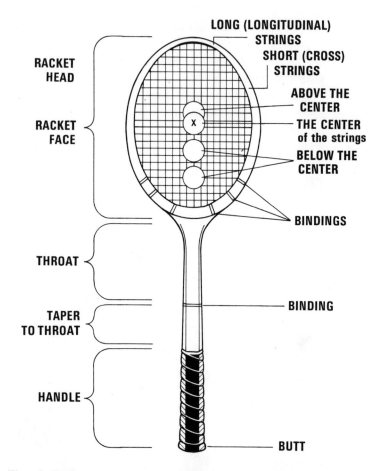

LONG (LONGITUDINAL) STRINGS

SHORT (CROSS) STRINGS

ABOVE THE CENTER

THE CENTER of the strings

BELOW THE CENTER

RACKET HEAD

RACKET FACE

THROAT

TAPER TO THROAT

HANDLE

BINDINGS

BINDING

BUTT

Illus. 1. Racket Terms: **RACKET HEAD**: the frame and strings. **RACKET FACE**: the whole surface of all the strings. The longitudinal strings are called the long strings; the cross ones sometimes called the short strings. **THROAT**: between strokes, the non-playing hand cradles the racket here. **TAPER TO THROAT**: from the top end of the grip, the handle tapers down to a flat throat. **BINDINGS**: they bind and decorate. **HANDLE**: sometimes called the grip. **BUTT**: the end of the handle or grip. **THE CENTER** of the strings: the center of the racket face, or the middle of the racket, or center, or middle.

2. HOW TO WATCH AND CONTROL THE BALL

THE RACKET has a large face, but don't let that mislead you. Except for an odd fluke, only the center or a little above it is any use to you. (See Illus. 1.) This is a small area. Therefore, to hit the ball properly you *need* to watch it. You're probably tired of hearing this, but if you don't already know, I will tell you *how* to watch it.

Watch the ball the whole distance. This makes it seem slower and easier to hit in the center of your racket. Suddenly remembering to watch it for the last few yards it travels does not give you the same comfortable feeling, and it will make your own shot hurried instead of smooth. Watch the ball come from your opponent's racket and from his side of the net. Nod your head slightly to it as it bounces, and smoothly follow it up. You may not see it hit your own strings, but you should watch it as far as you comfortably can.

Second, be conscious of watching the ball. As soon as you forget, you will not be watching it properly—that is, for the whole distance. When you know you are watching it, it looks clearer and perhaps even bigger.

If you watch your opponent's drive closely enough, you will see the ball bounce to its full height, drop just a fraction, and then seem to settle there for a moment as though it were a large golf ball on a giant tee. See if you can get that feeling. For

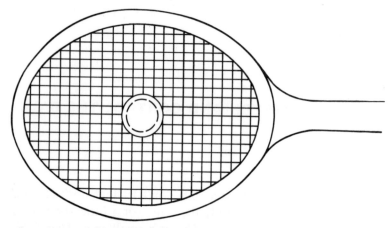

Illus. 2. LONG CONTACT. Flatten the ball against your strings. The ball goes almost straight, and with control.

if you do, you will be satisfied that watching the ball properly is always worth-while. After all, what more could you ask for than having the ball almost teed up?

You have heard it said that some player or other has a "good eye for a ball." You will too, if you do two things: watch the ball the whole way and know you are watching. It doesn't matter whether or not you can read small print or if you wear glasses. We are talking tennis, not optics.

Ball Control

You must have ball control, and you can. People who have played for years and who are still wild or unsafe have never learned *how*.

The great secret is long contact between ball and strings. If the ball were made of putty you would get wonderfully long contact and great ball control. It isn't, so your drive must feel as though you have collected the ball on the strings and are holding it flattened and stuck to them for as long as possible.

Then you send it on its way with the strings following closely: as if they did not wish to part with it. (See Illus 2.)

To hit the ball a sharp smack and simply let it go is trusting to luck instead of holding control with your strings. (See Illus. 3.)

For ball control you have to *feel* that the ball is going over the net and into the court from the moment it finally leaves your strings. You will not have a ball-control feeling if you merely hit the ball and then watch to see how it fares as it gets near the opposite backline. All you get that way is a praying feeling if the shot wasn't too bad and will be close to the line, or a disgusted one if it was terrible.

Topspin

You have probably heard of "topspin," and you may have thought it was the secret of ball control. Topspin makes the ball dip downwards, because the ball spins or rotates *forwards:* The air friction against the top surface of the ball is greater than the friction against its lower surface, so the ball dips. (See

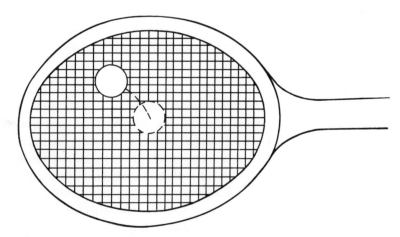

Illus. 3. HIT, BUT NO THOUGHT. Here the ball merely jumps off the strings.

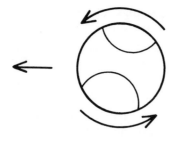

Illus. 4. TOPSPIN ON BALL. When a ball spins forward it must curve downward in its forward line of flight.

Illus. 4.) That is the physical result, but topspin is still not the basis of ball control.

"Why not?" you ask. "If a ball dips and lands within bounds instead of going over the baseline, isn't that ball control?"

It is, but only partial ball control. Look at it this way: the more spin you put on a ball, the less sure you can be of exactly where it will land. The secret of ball control is *long contact* rather than maximum topspin. However, topspin gives a measure of long contact, and we will speak of its other major benefits on page 37. The action of rolling the ball across the short strings of your racket gives it a longer contact than that thoughtless on-the-strings, off-the-strings smack I spoke of before. (See Illus. 5.)

Underspin

If you hit with underspin, the ball wants to stay up and go out—just the opposite of topspin. But you have noticed that players often use a cut or sliced stroke as a safety measure against a fast drive from an opponent. If this stroke is used for safety it must be connected with ball control. How then is underspin, which sends the ball up, a form of ball control?

The reason is that when you cut under the ball, it must—to some extent—travel across your short strings: and so you have some degree of long contact. (See Illus. 6.) In one form or

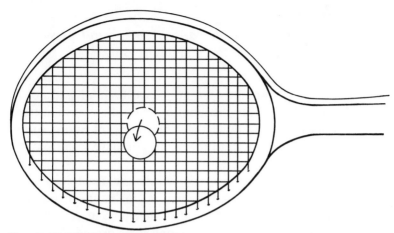

Illus. 5. TOPSPIN CONTACT. Roll the racket face over the ball across the short strings, and spin it forward. The ball curves downward, or dips. The ball is illustrated as having rolled a fraction down the short strings before leaving them.

NOTE: Illus. 5 and 6 are trying to portray the ball moving fractionally across the short strings. You do not hit the ball twice; that is a "double-hit" or "carry" and is a foul shot.

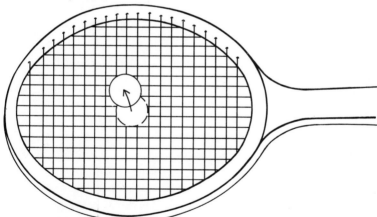

Illus. 6. UNDERSPIN CONTACT. Slice under the ball across the short strings and spin it backward. The ball hangs or sails. The ball is illustrated as having slid a fraction up the short strings before leaving them.

another, *long contact is the basis of ball control.* If you are playing badly, remember this and return to it.

Speed

At one time or another you may have been advised not to knock the cover off every ball, but to play with control instead. This would make you think that control means hitting softly, but this bears no relation to the tennis you have seen from the champions.

The way to hit a ball is *firmly.* Watch the champions again and note how firmly they hit the ball. At the moment you can't have their speed (nor did they, when they were at your present level), but you can start by emulating their firmness.

If you want to throw a ball very straight you don't balloon it (and you don't hurl it wildly at full strength): you throw firmly. *And* you keep the ball in your fingers as long as possible. Firmness and long contact—that's what you want.

3. GRIPS

For someone who is very young and too weak to swing a racket properly, the best grip would be two-handed. You should not adopt this grip. It has been tried by a number of champions over the last 40 years and it has spoiled their singles-game to a noticeable extent by shortening their reach. If you are already a two-handed player, take this much comfort: Because a two-handed stroke is strong in itself, you should have at least one good shot, and that is better than none at all. Who knows, you may become a famous doubles-player one day.

Again, if someone is so small that the net is too high for him and all the balls bounce higher than his shoulder, most of his strokes will have to be overhead pats. A suitable grip would be for him to have his forefinger up behind the racket handle.

It's different for you: Instead of being forced to use some makeshift method, you can adopt a proven orthodox grip. Let's see how you arrive at it, taking the forehand as a start.

Waist-high Grip

The center of the net is about waist-high to most people, so the easiest shot is a waist-high stroke with your racket about parallel to the ground. Stand sideways to the net. With your non-playing hand, hold your racket where the wood meets the leather and hold the racket out well in front of the middle of your waist. The short strings will point straight down (that is,

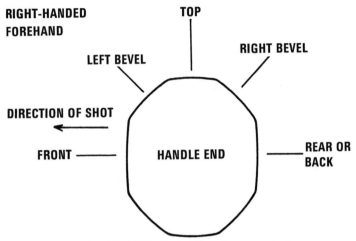

RIGHT-HANDED FOREHAND

TOP

LEFT BEVEL

RIGHT BEVEL

DIRECTION OF SHOT

FRONT —————

HANDLE END

REAR OR BACK

Illus. 7. HANDLE SURFACES. Racket face is square to the net.

the racket face will be square to the net). The handle should be pointing towards your navel. Take hold of the leather grip with your playing hand, and that is your grip.

It makes sense. You can see that all you will have to do to play natural forehands is to watch the ball, turn sideways to the net, take as many balls as you can waist-high, and stroke them past the net with long contact.

Variations

You will want to know why everyone does not use this clearly sensible grip. Why do champions, who know everything about tennis, play with different forehand grips?

Well, they all play their forehands with grips that are fairly similar to one another and they all base their individual grips on the idea I have just given. Assuming all players to be standing sideways to the net, here are the small differences: In hitting the ball waist-high with a flat racket face (that is, with the racket face square to the net), some players find it natural to make contact with the ball at a spot opposite the middle of their waists as I said. But some find it more natural to hit the ball from a point opposite their front hip (the hip nearer the net). Others hit a little *ahead* of this hip, and still others like to hit the ball from somewhere between the middle of their waists and their rear hips.

For a right-hander to hit the ball from opposite his front hip with a flat racket face (instead of from opposite his middle) he has to move his grip a little clockwise (to the right) on the handle. To hit the ball from nearer his rear hip, he has to move his hand a little to the left. This is the reason that players' grips vary by a small amount. It is time now to look at Illus. 7, showing the names used in describing the handle's surfaces, and at Illus. 8 to 12, demonstrating the small grip-variations just mentioned. Try them yourself. These illustrations also explain names that you may have heard used to describe various champions' forehand grips.

Your Own Grip

Which of these five waist-high grips is best for you? Whichever one feels most comfortable. Any slight difference *within* this range will not hinder the development of anyone's game, from beginner to champion, so you can be well satisfied with whatever becomes your own grip. What *would* be likely to hinder you is adopting a grip *outside* the range shown, in either direction: hand too much on top of the handle (your forehand grip is then likely to be weak) or hand too far behind handle (the change to your backhand grip will then be too large, and left-handers in particular should beware of this pitfall).

Cover the Handle

There was a reason for my saying you should hold your racket well out in front of you and about parallel to the ground when you take your grip: It gives you a grip with the handle

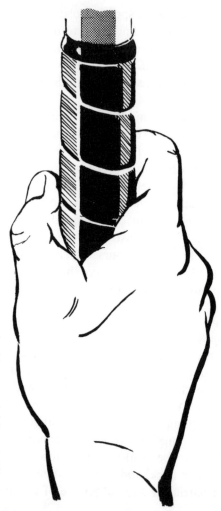

Illus. 8. AUSTRALIAN FOREHAND GRIP. Forehand grip to use when meeting the ball opposite the middle of your waist.

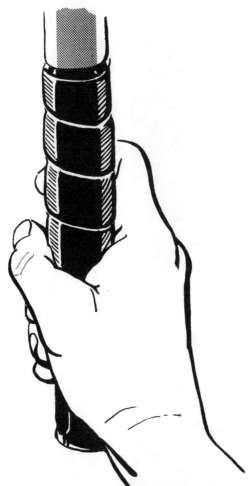

Illus. 9. EASTERN FOREHAND GRIP. Opposite your hip.

In these drawings do not view the racket as being upright, like a post. It is parallel to the ground, and you are looking down at the handle's top surface and two beveled surfaces. The short strings are pointing straight down and the racket face is square to the net. Your forehand grip can look something like any of the illustrations numbered 8, 9 and 10.

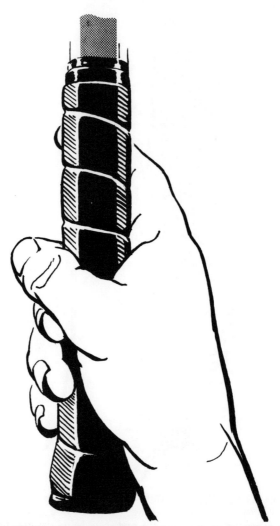

Illus. 10. EASTERN FOREHAND GRIP. A little in front of your hip.

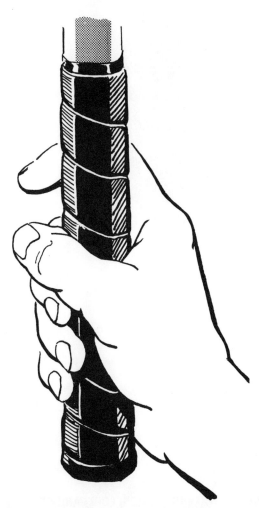

Illus. 11. EXTREME EASTERN FOREHAND GRIP. If your grip is any farther behind the handle than this (that is, if your thumb and forefinger V is farther to the right), you will have trouble with low and wide balls. The change to an adequate backhand grip already needs a large turn—left-handers in particular should beware.

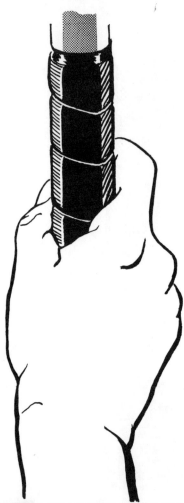

Illus. 12. CONTINENTAL (OR ENGLISH) FOREHAND GRIP. If your palm is even more on the top surface of the handle than this (that is, if your thumb and forefinger V is farther to the left), your forehand will not have much strength against a high ball. The Continental grip shown may become your eventual service grip. If may also be your backhand grip, though probably with the thumb and forefinger V turned a little more to the left on the handle and with the thumb advanced.

running diagonally across your hand. This means your hand and fingers will cover more of the handle than if you bunch your forefinger close up to the other three fingers. A spread grip gives you more strength to control your racket head.

If you are just beginning to play tennis there is no need for you to use the full length of the racket handle. Start short-handled—with your grip a little way from the end—if you feel you can manage better from there. You will use a longer handle as you gain control and confidence.

Backhand Grip

Like the forehand, the easiest backhand stroke is waist-high. You can find your backhand grip without trouble. Stand side-ways to the net with your playing arm nearer to the net this time. Hold your racket with your non-playing hand so that the racket face is square to the net. But don't point the handle towards your navel this time, because a backhand hit from this position would be too weak. Point it instead to a spot a good 6 inches or more ahead of your front hip—that is, 6 inches closer to the net than the hip you have nearer the net.

Keep the racket face square to the net and take your back-hand grip. Notice that your hand is more on the top surface of the handle than it was with your forehand grip. (You will see this for yourself at your first try.) Next, put your thumb diagonally across (not straight along) the back surface of the handle. This is support for the weak opening there was a moment ago between your forefinger and thumb. Most people place the thumb this way, but some feel they get a tighter grip of the handle if their thumb is round it. Do not bunch your fingers and place your thumb straight along the rear surface. This makes your grip too stiff for freedom.

An adequate grip is so important a part of producing a sound backhand that we will return to it in more detail in the Back-hand chapter. Meanwhile, please see Illus. 13.

Illus. 13. ADEQUATE BACKHAND GRIP.

Service Grip

Use your forehand grip while you are learning to serve and keep to this grip until you have a reliable serve. After that, but not until your serve is really safe, you should begin to move your serving grip little by little to the left. Illus. 12 shows the type of grip you should eventually use for your serve: the Continental grip. (Should it happen to be the grip you use for your forehand, then use it for your serve as well.)

Why should you use this "Continental" grip for serving? Because, later, you can get more whip into your service this way, like wrist action in throwing a ball. Why not start this way? Because you probably won't be able to manage it at first and, instead, you might develop some freak action.

Girls do not throw with as much snap as boys, and so a girl's forehand grip generally remains her best serving grip.

Tightness

How tightly do you grip all your grips? The answer is the same as the description given for ideal speed: grip firmly and strongly as you come forward to meet the ball. A loose hold is no good either for meeting a fast ball or for-controlling the racket head to be exactly in the right place. On the other hand, do not try to "squeeze water out of the handle" (especially while you are taking your racket back) or you will be clumsy and stiff. One of the good things about tennis is that, within certain limits, it is a natural game.

Let's now look at the strokes you are going to make.

4. FOREHAND

YOUR MAIN STROKE is your forehand. Develop it first and do not lose it while gaining other strokes. The forehand is the easiest stroke to learn and the one most likely to go astray later. Get it and always keep it solid. Later, after you have finished practicing other strokes, you should always end your practices with some forehands.

You may think the serve the most important stroke because it must be part of every point. However, you use your serve in only half the games and your forehand in every one. Also, you serve only once (perhaps twice) for every point, but in each point you may hit a dozen forehands. Your serve is more restricted. It has to land in one small square of the whole court where your opponent is waiting for it, and from where he usually returns it. This usually brings your forehand into play again—and you have the whole of your opponent's court to use.

Perhaps you think the volley (playing the ball before it bounces) is more important, because you have seen champions play a serve-and-volley game on a fast court surface. Well, watch the champions playing again (which I will repeatedly be asking you to do). This time, take note that if each player did not have a good forehand he would be almost helpless every time his opponent had the net position. Whenever the court surface is slow—that is, composed of clay, which gives a slower bounce than grass or an indoor court—you will see more forehands than volleys from champions, even from those with big serves.

Early concentration on your forehand does not mean you will develop lopsided groundstrokes—that is, a strong forehand and weak backhand. Lopsidedness often results from a player's using a forehand grip too far round the handle from his backhand grip and then having insufficient time to change to an adequate backhand grip when he has to play his backhand shots. A strong forehand will not interfere with your backhand. You need it. Without it you are rather like a hunter without a gun.

"Be a Forehand"

For a young player starting out, it is not at all a bad idea to "Be a Forehand" on court. You can learn your other strokes one after another and play them as necessary. But, meanwhile, whenever an ordinary sort of ball lands in front of you or out to your right side (or to your left side if you are a left-hander), all strain is off and you and your forehand are ready to play it. You may be surprised to know that there are many apparently good players about who seem to have all the strokes in the game, and yet the forehand is their least confident shot.

Later you will acquire all the strokes and play them naturally. You may, for instance, develop a strong serve-and-volley game on fast courts. But in gathering all this sophistication, your forehand should remain your basic and most trusted shot: always reliable and capable of attack. It should be something an opponent tries to stay clear of. If you neglect this shot in the glamour of others you will make the mistake of your tennis life.

A strong forehand is the key to your having an effective and attacking return-of-service. On the other hand, if your forehand is weak it becomes the easiest of targets—because, as we shall see later, the easiest serve a right-hander can make is to his opponent's forehand side in the first court.

Your Forehand

What of the basic stroke itself? You've had most of it already, possibly without realizing it. You know that you should have a waist-high swing, matching the height of the net. You have a grip that meets the ball comfortably somewhere between your hips or just in front of your front hip. You know to watch the ball the whole of its flight towards you. You know to turn sideways to the net and aim the ball firmly with long contact. You also know that the forehand can practically make you as a tennis player. In short, you know a lot. And you need to know it instinctively, because you can't figure things out while a fast ball is coming at you.

Similarly, you should picture your forehand as a complete and co-ordinated stroke. You are not likely to get this idea of smoothness from photographs. It is far better for you to watch a good player playing singles, where many forehands are played without haste. Watch him turn easily into his sideways-to-the-net position, take the ball waist-high, and stroke it smoothly and firmly across the net. A living and moving model is what you want.

An old saying is to be sure you're right, then forge ahead. In playing your forehand it will add greatly to your naturalness and confidence if you take note of the points set out below.

SWING. Start your backswing early—as distinct from, say, running over to a wide ball with your racket by your side and then hurriedly starting your swing after you reach the ball. A swing in line with your shoulders with your body sideways to the net, is as far back as you need go. Take your racket back about in line with the height of the ball's bounce. Your swing can be straight back and straight forward, or it can be in the form of a flat loop. Firm up your grip as you swing forward. Don't jerk. Stroke firmly instead.

CONTACT. Long. *Feel* that the ball is already on its correct path over the net and into court.

Illus. 14. FOREHAND: Hitting across the front leg.

FOLLOW-THROUGH. Regard this as part of your long contact. When your racket is pointing towards the net there is no need for your follow-through to carry on any farther. The ball has long since gone on its way.

FOOTWORK AND WEIGHT. When you are making things easy for someone smaller and weaker whom you are not trying to beat (a practice game, for instance, in which you play the part of instructor) you keep the ball nicely short for him. If you were pitted against a strong player and trying to win, you too would like to receive the ball nice and short. In competition, your opponent won't put it there for you, so you have to use your feet to get behind the ball and come forward—as though his shot had been short all the time. This amounts to having good footwork and using your weight well. It is as simple as that. Notice, by the way, how a good player repeatedly gets behind the ball; he turns an apparently good shot from his opponent into a short ball, and hits it strongly.

FOOT PLACEMENT. To aim straight, you must be sideways to the net. When the ball is short, advance your front foot (left foot for a right-hander) towards the ball. When the ball is wide, there are two ways to reach it with your body still in the proper position. Either move your left foot to the ball and hit "across" your left leg. Or move your right foot behind the ball and then advance your left and hit "along" your leg. (See Illus. 14 and 15.) Both methods are correct, and you will see champions using both. You are thus perfectly correct in being natural, using your feet freely. However:

Do *not* finish your stroke with your weight still on your right foot.

Do *not* stand square to the net.

Do *not* forget to get your front leg in place to take your weight.

If you miss on any of these counts, your shot will be weak, or your aim will be crooked, or your balance will be lost.

TIMING. Nearly all timing mistakes are made by swinging

Illus. 15. FOREHAND: Hitting along the front leg.

forward a fraction too early, not too late. The reason is that you imagine your racket head travels at the same speed throughout your forward swing. It doesn't. Just before meeting the ball, the racket head travels faster than you would have thought—in catching up with your wrist, which has led the racket head by a little. If you do not allow for this short period of extra speed, your racket tends to arrive too early. To time the stroke correctly, you must not start late, nor should you stop the swing and start it again. You simply train yourself, mentally, to delay your stroke a fraction. Whether you take the racket straight back or in a shallow loop, take a mental pause for a fraction of a second before swinging forward. That's all it takes.

Concentrate on these points one at a time if you like, but you will find they all flow into one co-ordinated stroke—your forehand.

Forehand Spin

You cannot watch a good player hitting his forehand without noticing that he often spins the ball. You need to understand exactly what you are seeing and how to apply it to your own forehand. Forehand spin is fairly simply explained.

In the first place, every forehand you hit will put some amount of spin on the ball, whether it be small or large. At this comment you immediately say, "What about a flat drive?"

Well, there is no such thing as a perfectly flat drive. You may hit the ball with a flat racket face, but your swing and the racket face itself rise as you hit the ball. And this gives the ball a small amount of forward spin. Get your racket out and make a slow-motion forehand against a ball held out in your left hand, and you will see what I mean.

The term "flat drive" exists, however, and rightly so. In making this stroke you mentally concentrate on long contact, squashing the ball against the strings of your racket as you send it deep to the opposite backline with more accuracy of aim than any other forehand can give you. You don't have to think about the spin. The small amount that is there, is forward spin (akin to topspin, but having less spin). Therefore this forward spin is acting to your advantage by bringing the ball down a little shorter than the point you aimed for, without your even thinking about it. In other words, although the flat drive physically puts a little spin on the ball, we need think of it only as a flat forehand. As such it is a distinct stroke in its own right and is correctly called a flat drive.

Topspin Again—and Why

You need to have a topspin drive. You need to be able to make the ball dip and land soon after it has crossed the net. Here is an example. Your opponent is at the net. You try to angle the ball past him. You manage to put the ball beyond his reach, but it lands beyond the sideline as well and you lose the point. The next time this situation occurs, to keep the ball inside the sideline, you hit it slower—and he reaches it. Topspin will solve your dilemma. You can hit the ball firmly and make it drop quickly enough to land inside the sideline.

To hit with topspin, start your forward swing a little below the height of the bounce of the ball (not too far below or you will lift the ball too much and hit it out) and roll the short strings of your racket strongly over the top of the ball. Some players say their strings first contact the ball slightly below its center, while others insist that to them topspin means wiping their short strings across the top half of the ball. This shows us that players may have a different idea about a stroke and yet get the same result: namely, spinning the ball forward so that it curves downward. The point is that you must develop your own topspinning grip of your strings on the ball's cover. No one else can do it for you. I can tell you about it and a coach

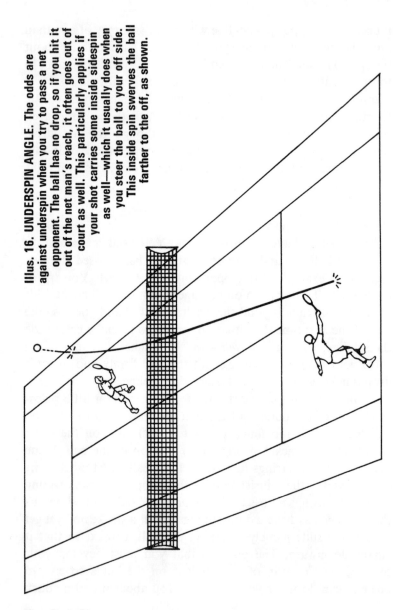

Illus. 16. UNDERSPIN ANGLE. The odds are against underspin when you try to pass a net opponent. The ball has no drop, so if you hit it out of the net man's reach, it often goes out of court as well. This particularly applies if your shot carries some inside sidespin as well—which it usually does when you steer the ball to your off side. This inside spin swerves the ball farther to the off, as shown.

can demonstrate it, but you have to get it by yourself—on your own racket strings.

A number of champions, including Rod Laver, have been famous for their use of topspin. As well as using it repeatedly, they sometimes cram what we could call "heavy topspin" on the ball: *really* making it dip. The ball can be driven either sharply across court or forced to dip down at an opponent's shoelaces.

Nevertheless, topspin is not the answer to everything. It tends to make your drive land too short, thus making things easy for an opponent at the baseline. Also, when you try for a lot of topspin, it is easy to mis-hit the ball.

Underspin in Detail

So that you will understand not to base your forehand on any form of underspin, I will put its bad points first.

Underspin makes the ball spin backwards as it travels through the air. Since its lower surface has more friction against the air than its top surface, the ball sails. Where a topspin forehand may have landed well inside the baseline and a flat drive safely in, an underspin forehand of similar speed would tend to just miss the backline. "Bad luck," someone watching might say, but the truth is that the odds are against underspin for good length (that is, landing the ball deep, near the baseline).

The odds are even worse when you use underspin in trying to angle a shot past a net player. The situation is similar to the one described a moment ago when we were discussing the need for topspin, but worse. (See Illus. 16.) Further, an underspin shot is the easiest type of ball for your opponent to volley, because the ball sails so straight. It could well be called a "sitting duck."

Take care that underspin does not become an unnoticed part of your forehand. Many players think they are hitting flat when they are really slicing under the ball a little. They aim, and the

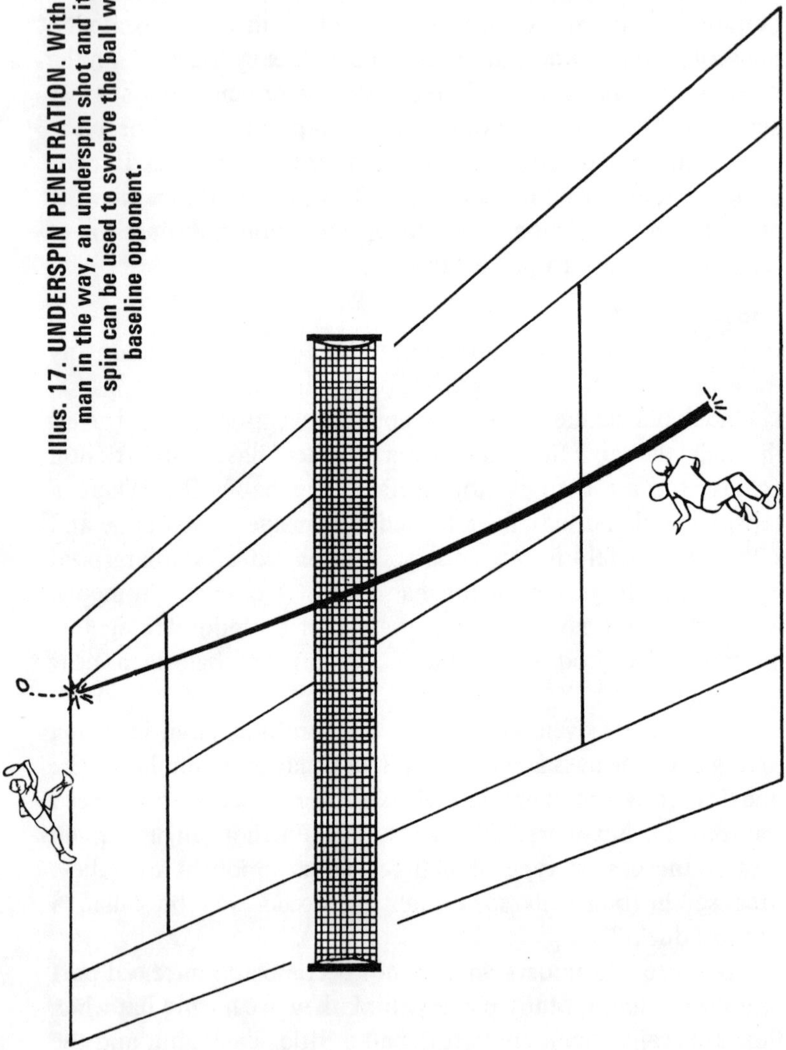

Illus. 17. UNDERSPIN PENETRATION. With no net man in the way, an underspin shot and its inside spin can be used to swerve the ball wide of a baseline opponent.

ball goes farther than they meant—not landing right on the spot (or a little short of it) like a flat forehand, nor much more safely short of the backline like a topspin drive.

Finally, underspin makes the ball-bounce slower and, normally, easier for your opponent.

That is the case against basing your forehand drive on underspin. However, underspin itself has some good points or no one would use it. Here they are.

Shots called "cuts" or "slices" consist mainly of underspin. Their other component is some degree of sidespin. Such shots are often used as a safety measure against an opponent's fast drive. They are safe for two reasons. One is that the stroke itself has only a short swing, which makes timing easy. The other is that there is a measure of long contact here, since all spin-shots travel across your strings to some extent.

Also, you can clear the net with more ease and certainty if you cut under a very low ball. Similarly, when a ball bounces too high for you to drive with comfort, you can hit it downward with a slice. This may be mainly sidespin, but there is also some underspin to it—certainly no topspin.

Hitting slightly inside the ball with underspin can provide a swerving penetration to your baseline opponent's backhand corner. (See Illus. 17.)

Do Not Overdo Spin

You can see that if you found your forehand on topspin, you at least have some of the odds working for you. If you found it on underspin, however, your opponents have only to take the net to have you at their mercy. What if you were to concentrate on spin alone, all forms of it? Would that be the answer to becoming safe and firm? No, because you would have to give up the proven basic value of aiming straight with long contact. And from this one proven skill, clean hitting, good timing and use of weight, and more and more speed in your strokes will all gradually come as your game develops.

If you based your forehand on using some form of spin for every ball, you would be liable to mis-hit far too many balls. You would be forever hitting across the ball's line of flight, first in one direction and then in another. You would never be aiming, but always adjusting instead. Finally, you would never advance to the standard of play which firm speed and a basically straight aim will give you. In short, although a little spin comes into all your forehands, spin itself should be an addition to this stroke and not its basis.

Essentials for Your Own Forehand

You have your own comfortable waist-high grip.

You watch the ball the *whole* way. You let it reach the top of its bounce and begin to settle. This is its slowest spot, for a tennis player's purpose. Perhaps it may lose more of its forward speed as it drops farther, but it will then be falling at a greater angle to the path of your sideways-to-the-net, hip-to-hip forward swing. And it will therefore be less easy to hit. A ball that drops some distance at an angle will not give you the feeling of having it teed-up and ready to hit.

You turn sideways to the net and make your backswing early. You take your racket back only as far as you need in order to stroke the ball firmly and aim it straight. You firm your grip as you swing forward. You hold the ball on the strings in long contact, regarding your follow-through as part of this long contact.

You aim to play as many forehands as possible with your racket about parallel to the ground and the ball comfortably waist-high. When the ball is lower, *bend your knees and bring your waist down to the ball*—and again you can swing a parallel racket. Do not stand up straight and let the racket head incline down below your wrist. That makes you lob the ball up, rather than sweep it across the net.

When the ball bounces high, go back and then come forward to the ball, converting it to a waist-high forehand. If there is no time to go back and you must play the ball at a high bounce, take your racket back high, about in line with the height you will hit the ball.

If the ball is waist-high but rising, don't cringe below it. Stand tall.

We will return to your forehand when we come to Practice (Chapter 7). Meanwhile, to the other side: your backhand.

5. BACKHAND

YOU MUST HAVE a backhand. In the early days of your tennis you may be able to run round a lot of your opponent's shots and play them with your forehand. But as the standard of your opponents improves (along with yours) their shots will become firmer and more accurate, and you will no longer have time to step round them. If your forehand has been likened to a hunter's gun, playing with no backhand is like having one hand tied behind your back.

Your backhand, probably more than any other of your strokes, is founded on grip. Your backhand grip must be firm and must give you a feeling of strength. After that, it should be as flexible as possible. Please refer once more to Illus. 13, to see what an adequate backhand grip looks like. Now let me explain what is meant by its being both firm and flexible. You can follow these two requirements in a practical manner if you get your racket out as you look at the illustration and follow the text.

FIRMNESS. Hold your racket in a backhand grip with the *V* made by your thumb and forefinger lying on about the center of the rear surface of the handle. Bunch your fingers and place your thumb straight along this rear surface. Grip hard. You'll agree this grip is certainly firm. In fact, it's rocklike.

But it is not flexible enough for you. To have your arm

straight and the racket face square to the net, you would have to make contact with the ball as early as a full arm's length ahead (closer to the net) of your right hip. That's a long way farther out in front of your hip than the 6 inches or so we spoke about on page 27 when we briefly discussed your backhand grip. With such an inflexible grip, if you did not have time to meet the ball well in front of you, you would hit it into the side fence rather than over the net. Nor is this grip natural enough. Your racket does not feel a part of your arm. It is like a separate appliance, thrust out in front of your body instead of feeling co-ordinated with it in the manner shown in Illus. 13.

FLEXIBILITY. If you used a backhand grip that placed the thumb and forefinger V somewhere on the top surface of the handle (like most forehand grips), this would be very flexible because it would allow you to take the ball as far behind you as possible. But it would be woefully weak. Also, if you wanted to hit the ball when it was nearer to the net, your wrist would be awkwardly bent and would have no power.

An Adequate Backhand Grip

The heel of your hand (the fleshy pad in line with and below your little finger) should sit comfortably on the end of the top surface of the racket handle. The thumb-and-forefinger V is to fall on the left bevel of the racket handle or near the top of its rear surface. Your forefinger should extend a little to cover more handle, just as it does with your forehand grip. To match this forefinger-handle-cover, advance your thumb diagonally across the rear surface of the handle, at any angle comfortable to you. This thumb position gives your grip support and firmness when you meet the ball—and without being too rigid, as is the case with the "thumb straight along the back" grip.

Hold your racket out as if you were hitting an imaginary waist-high ball. You will see that for the racket face to be square to the net, it needs to meet this imaginary ball somewhere ahead of your front hip (that is, between your front hip and the net). But this contact point will not have to be at that full forward armstretch demanded by the very strong but inflexible backhand position. Please look once more at Illus. 13, this time as a combination of firmness and flexibility.

Changing from Forehand to Backhand Grip

This can be done quicker and more easily than you may have thought. The change takes place as you are taking your racket back in its backswing for your backhand stroke. By the time your racket is ready to swing forward you will have your backhand grip ready. Here's how it's done.

The technique is to use your non-playing hand to twist the racket a little to its backhand-grip position. Practice this first without a ball. Stand facing the net, holding your racket handle in your forehand grip and using your left-hand fingers and the ball of your left thumb to cradle the racket's throat. (See Illus. 1.) Imagine the ball is coming to your backhand side. Step forward and across with your right foot. Take the racket back with your left hand and in the same motion let the ball of your left thumb twist the throat slightly clockwise: You will find the handle has turned sufficiently and is ready to be held firmly in your backhand grip. Now swing forward to make your stroke.

Backhand Naturalness

You may not have realized it, but you are already naturally backhanded in some ways. How do you hit someone with your elbow? How do you deal cards? How do you toss rings?

Perhaps you knew about this backhand naturalness before. If not, it will increase your backhand confidence greatly.

After the work you have done on your forehand, learning the backhand is an easier task: For this time you have confidence

Illus. 18. BACKHAND—Hitting across the front leg.

in your sound grip, you already know to watch the ball, and you turn sideways to the net. You know, also, to hit waist-high as much as possible, and when the ball is low, you bend your knees to take your waist down to it. Finally, you use long contact and follow-through. It all develops very naturally.

Backhand Is Not an Identical Twin

You should be prepared for a few practical differences from your forehand:

GRIP. The backhand grip is stronger. You get more leverage from it. The forehand grip is more flexible: You can handle wider and more awkward shots from your opponent.

WATCHING THE BALL. You watch it better on the backhand

side. This is caused by your turning your head and shoulder round as you move to your sideways-to-the-net position. Instead of my describing this further, I recommend that you watch a number of players in action. You will see many of them lifting their heads as they hit a forehand. However, they keep their heads down longer, with a better sight of the ball, on their backhands. Remember to keep your own head down with your forehand as well as with your backhand.

TURNING SIDEWAYS TO THE NET. The backhand demands this. Otherwise your stroke will be pulled to your right side, across your body. From a square-on stance you may be able to prod or cut the ball, to some degree, in the direction you desire, but you will not be able to hit hard and straight. Left-handers in particular should take note.

FOOT PLACEMENT. Because turning fully sideways is essential for a good backhand shot, most players put their right foot to the ball and play "across the front leg." (See Illus. 18.) Watch, and you will notice that far more backhands are played across the right leg than are forehands across the left leg.

BACKSWING. On the forehand a shallow loop is permissible, even normal. On the backhand, however, take your racket straight back and then come straight forward. You do not need the momentum of a loop, because your backhand grip is strong in itself. You should not develop a looped backhand swing. It makes your timing difficult unnecessarily.

AIMING. Most players can aim their forehand about equally well across court (to their opponent's forehand), or down the sideline (to their opponent's backhand). With a backhand, cross-court is by far the more natural direction. To play a strong backhand down the line to your opponent's forehand, you can expect to have to turn your body more than sideways to the net. Again, left-handers should note this.

SPIN. Watching experienced players, you will have noticed

NET

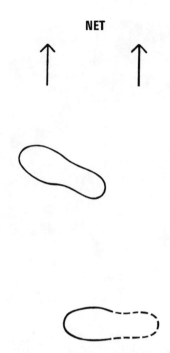

Illus. 19. STEPPING STRONGLY INTO YOUR BACKHAND. Your backhand is not likely to be as flexible as your forehand. You won't reach as far with it and cover so much court. Compensate by making it feel strong and solid. At all costs, avoid having a weak backhand, defenceless against attack.

that they slice or underspin their backhands much more often than their forehands. In fact, many players' basic game consists of a flat or topspin forehand and a sliced backhand. A backhand slice is normally stronger than a forehand slice, the reason lying in the leverage given by the backhand grip.

Nevertheless you cannot pass an opposing net-man as effectively with a slice of any sort as you can with topspin.

John Newcombe illustrates foot placement for a backhand lob across the front leg.

Exceptional players prove this rule, as always, with Ken Rosewall being the most exceptional of all.

SPEED. You gain more force on the backhand side than the forehand *for a backswing of equal length.* However, it is normal to use a longer swing when making a forehand stroke and therefore to have more speed at your command in forehand action than in backhand.

Playing Your Backhand

Prepare early for your backhand, because you are probably not so used to swinging from this side. Watch the ball. Take your racket back, bending your elbow to an *L* and changing grip as you do so with your left fingers and the ball of your thumb. Step out firmly towards the ball with your right foot— a good firm step, with your heels about a foot and a half apart, so that you feel solid. (See Illus. 19.) Bend your right knee and lean your right shoulder to the ball.

Keeping your head down, swing forward and hit the ball, straightening your arm at the moment of contact. Your racket should be about parallel to the ground. Use long contact and end your follow-through about in line with your right shoulder.

With these points in mind watch a good player's backhand in action.

You should now have the fundamentals of the backhand in your mind and in your mind's eye. There will be more advice in the Practice chapter.

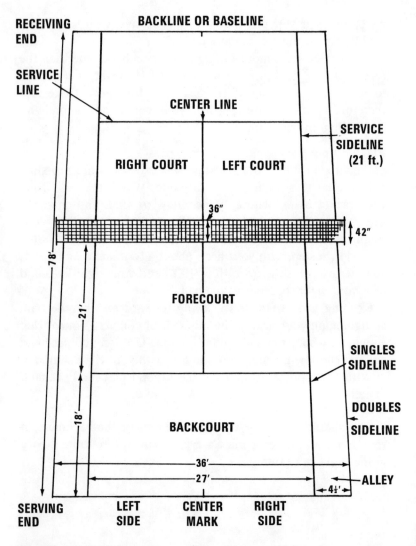

Illus. 20. COURT TERMS. You serve from both ends of the court, changing ends after the first game and all odd games. For simplicity, we will take the lower end of the diagram as the serving end.

6. SERVICE

First, let's look at Illus. 20—to get our terms straight. The first point and all odd points are served from right of the center mark. The second point and all even points are served from left of it. We speak of serving from the right side (or to the right court) and from the left side (or to the left court).

When we receive service on the first point, we are said to be "playing in the right court." This is also called the "first court," or the "forehand court," and sometimes the "deuce court." For the even-numbered points we play in the left, or "second," or "backhand," or "ad" court. Occasionally you may hear this court referred to as the "left-handers' court": "Court" is short for "service court," and from this comes the term "service box."

The serve has a lot of arm and racket action connected with it, but please do not imagine that learning to serve well is going to be complicated. A famous French player of long ago, Henri Cochet, was once asked exactly how he produced his service. "I throw the ball up," he said, "and then I hit it."

There's a little more to it than that, and I will give you the points step by step.

Grip

When learning to serve, begin by using your forehand grip,

whatever it may be. This makes you feel at home. Hold the handle a little short, if you want to.

I have already mentioned in the Grip chapter that you may serve with a different grip a little later. Perhaps you have even heard players talking of serving with a Continental grip, or, confusingly, with a backhand grip. We will straighten all this out by the end of this chapter, but right now let's get on with your serve.

Foot Placement

Please study Illus. 21. You line up the toes of your shoes with the exact spot in your opponent's court where you want your serve to land. This does not telegraph your intended aim to your receiving opponent: after all, he cannot see the exact position of your feet. To him, you merely seem to be standing sideways to the net.

In lining up for your service, your foot placement can always be perfect. Make it perfect, and use this precision as a reminder that, with this stroke alone, you can take your time. Far too many players hurry their serves, not now and then, but always.

Put your front foot about 2 inches behind the baseline, to avoid touching it and thereby foot-faulting. If you find you tend to shuffle your front foot a little as you serve, then make your clearance zone 4 inches or so.

Throwing the Ball Up

Before reading any further, please get two tennis balls and hold them in your left hand, and follow me through—acting out every step.

Don't cram the balls together: separate them—you are going to hit them one at a time. Hold the first one between the ball of your thumb and a point above the first joints of your (comfortably separated) forefinger and middle fingers. Hold the second ball against the lower part of your palm with your

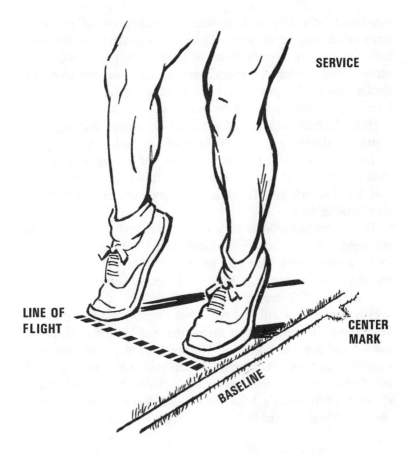

Illus. 21. SERVICE FOOT PLACEMENT. Line up the toes of your shoes with the intended direction of your serve.

third and little fingers. Keep this one safely out of the way, since when you serve you will be concentrating on the first ball. Do not get into the habit of holding only one ball when serving and leaving the other lying about. You are likely to sprain your ankle if you should accidentally step on it. Moreover, its presence disturbs your concentration.

Hold the balls in front of your left hip before starting your throw. In throwing a ball up, however, do not release it from as far down as that: this would make for a long and erratic throw. Instead, raise your hand higher than your head before you let the ball go. Try this now yourself, and develop a comfortable throw.

Throw the ball a little forward of your body and a little to the right. That is about where everyone would naturally want to hit a serve from. But you must throw the ball higher than you may have expected, because your racket should hit it with your arm at a full stretch upwards.

How high? You will find your own height when you practice your serve. In general, you throw the ball high enough for it to stop and begin to fall before your racket hits it with your arm stretched straight. Remember when you were playing your waist-high forehand and backhand and you let the ball reach the crest of its bounce, then settle—and *then* you hit it? This is similar. When the arc feels comfortable and safe, you have it right.

Are You Left-Handed?

If you are a left-hander, you will have had no trouble so far: Where I have written "left" you will simply have been holding the balls in your right hand and in front of your right hip, and so on. But I want to make something clear right now: Don't do what a right-hander does: That is, don't start learning to serve from the right side (serving into the right court). As a left-hander, you should learn to serve from the left side (serving into the left court). Unless you do this, what I have to say about natural swerve or curve in serving will make no sense.

Also, you may as well know now that neither your wrist nor shoulder nor anything else is made differently. However, left-handers develop certain characteristics in tennis, and I will go into these for you in some detail in Chapter 11. Now, right-handers and left-handers alike, let's turn to your service action.

Shoulder Serve

Stand to the right of the center mark (left-handers, stand to the left of it), line up the toes of your shoes, bend your right elbow up sharply, and hold your right wrist somewhere near your right shoulder. (Left-handers, you know what to do.) Throw the ball up with your free hand. Now, straightening your elbow, serve the ball.

With this simple method, little could cause you to develop a faulty action. However, if you find you haven't enough power to hit the ball smoothly over the net, then move several yards *inside* the baseline and serve smoothly from there. Do not be too proud to do this because, after all, you are only using a shortened or restricted serving action. You are only serving from your shoulder. Your purpose at the start is to get a plain and smooth action that feels comfortable and gives you confidence. You must not jerk at the ball or strain to get it over the net. If necessary, go right up to the service line to learn this shoulder serve *smoothly*.

Natural Swerve

You should not try to slice the ball. You will be hitting with a more or less flat stroke, but nevertheless you will be able to feel a trace of swerve in your service, even if you cannot see it. This swerve comes from the slight slice that the forehand grip you are using will give the ball, and from your serving somewhat diagonally, from right side to your opponent's right court (left-handers, serve from the left side to your opponent's left court).

This swerve is a server's friend and ally, for control. Once your serve has crossed the net, its natural swerve, however slight, gives the ball a longer path to travel and so it has more chance of landing inside the service box. (See Illus. 22.)

At this stage, do not try to develop a widely swinging curve or you will mis-hit and spoil the smoothness you must have. Instead, be aware of the small controlling swerve that naturally comes into your serve, even at this stage—and feel some self-satisfaction over it.

Take It Easy

Practice this shoulder serve again and again, mainly aiming for the farthest diagonal corner of the right court. Do not be satisfied if you are only lobbing or lofting the ball over the net. Move inside the baseline; if necessary, serve from closer and closer to the net until you feel you are hitting the ball smoothly past the net instead of lobbing it over. You must feel that you are aiming the ball with long contact into the service box—not lobbing it, not forcing it. Practice until you can hit it smoothly from the baseline and into court. Take as much time as you like in reaching this stage. Rome wasn't built in a day.

Left Side

When you are reasonably satisfied with your serving to the right court (left-handers to the left court) with that feeling of aim, long contact and slight swerve (even if you cannot yet do it properly from as far back as the baseline)—then try serving from the other side. Here you may experience a little disappointment, because you will not get the same sensation of swerve. Instead, you may feel you are *patting* the ball to the off side. Do not mind. If you and your opponent are both right-handed (or both left-handed), at least you are serving towards his backhand.

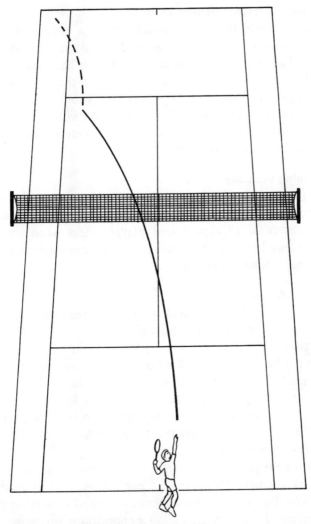

Illus. 22. SERVICE—NATURAL SWERVE: Slight swerve is an ally. After the ball has crossed the net, its swerve gives it a longer path to travel before landing. This increases your serve's chance of being right instead of perhaps just out.

Dropping the Racket Behind Your Back

When you feel that your shoulder serve is comfortable, the next stage is to drop your racket head down behind your back and start your serve from there. If you had only enough shoulder-serve power to serve from inside the baseline, the extra swing of serving from down behind your back may give you the power that was lacking before. You will not, however, have wasted your time in practicing the simple shoulder serve and learning to aim smoothly.

Developing the Loop

In dropping your racket head down behind your back more and more rhythmically, you will develop the loop that you see in the serves of all experienced players. And when you are ready to lengthen your swing still more, you can start it with the racket head down by your foot.

Complete Action

We now come to the final stage, which gives you the service action you see most experienced players use. Hold the racket against the balls in front of your left hip. As your left hand throws the ball up, your racket head sweeps down to your feet, rises in a loop behind your back and stretches up to hit the ball at arm's length. It hits the ball with aim, long contact and swerve, then curves its follow-through down towards your left side. The whole action is like throwing a ball—or like throwing your racket over the net.

Building up your serve *by stages* is essential. It prevents you from unknowingly developing a freak action. And at all these stages you are closer to a champion's method of serving than you realize. Mostly a champion concentrates on lining up, throwing accurately, and aiming smoothly with long contact (automatically, of course). That is exactly what you have been doing, except with more conscious effort. You would not have thought of any of these things if you had tried to copy the complete service action of a champion all at one shot.

Advanced Serving

Even though you know the secret of the champion's graceful, seemingly one-motion serves, you still have plenty of work to do on your own unpolished serve at this stage. Nevertheless, you will want to know the elements of advanced serving so that you can recognize them when you watch advanced players in action.

You can get more wrist-snap, as in throwing a ball, if you use a grip that places your thumb and forefinger V on the left bevel (identified in Illus. 7) of the racket handle rather than on the top surface. Please refer back to Illus. 12. If this happens to be the forehand grip you use, then you have already been serving with the advanced serving grip just mentioned. This will have done no harm. However, most players use a forehand grip with the V somewhere on the top surface of the handle (Illus. 7), so the advanced service (or Continental) grip generally comes as a change.

If you start with the advanced service grip you are likely to hook your serves into the side fence. And girls who try this grip first-off will probably not get enough power and weight behind the ball. In either case, your attempts at compensation are likely to give you a freak action. And freak actions hinder your future development in both accuracy and speed.

When you have built up to your full service swing, or close to it, you can begin changing little by little to the V on the left-bevel grip. Many girls find that no matter how much skill they acquire, their forehand grip remains their best service grip. They find it steadier and stronger and are content to leave the wrist-snapping to the men.

Slice, Flat, Topspin

Please look at Illus. 23. The serve that you are building up by stages, with the help of this chapter, is a slice serve. You throw the ball up to about the same position as the slice throw in the sketch: that is, a little to your right. The player illustrated has the advanced service grip and is going to slice round the ball more than you have been doing, giving it more out-curve (that is, a curve away from a right-handed receiver's forehand).

When a server throws the ball above his head instead of to his right, he can no longer slice round it. From this position he can hit it flat. This can give a server his fastest ball, because there is no spin to slow it down and because it will travel in a straight line with no delaying curve. So flat serves are used as cannonball serves. If a fast straight serve is to land in your opponent's court it must clear the net by only a few inches, unless it is hit from a great height. Therefore, effective cannonball serving is restricted to men who are very tall.

From the same overhead position of the thrown-up ball, that is, the one above the server's head (the middle ball in Illus. 23) the server can hit the back of the ball with an upward motion of his racket. Pictures or description are not good enough; you must watch someone do it. The upward contact of strings brushing upwards and over the ball gives it topspin. This means the ball can go fairly high over the net and drop safely in play, like a topspin forehand. When mastered, this topspin serve is generally safer than a slice serve, because it can drop quickly into the service box. However, it is not so accurate for placement.

The third position, when the ball is thrown slightly over to the left, allows a right-handed server to use maximum topspin and thus arc the ball high over the net. It also kicks up, on bouncing. Girls, incidentally, seldom bother with this serve.

I shall not take you any further away from your own game. You have a lot of work to do. It is time for Practice.

Illus. 23. TYPES OF SERVICE.

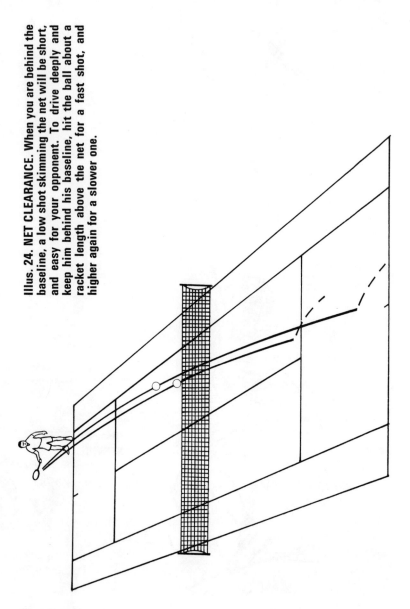

Illus. 24. NET CLEARANCE. When you are behind the baseline, a low shot skimming the net will be short, and easy for your opponent. To drive deeply and keep him behind his baseline, hit the ball about a racket length above the net for a fast shot, and higher again for a slower one.

7. PRACTICE

PRACTICE IS NOT REALLY WORK. There can be as much fun in practicing as in playing a match. It's a great thrill to win a match, but you get great satisfaction in practice when you suddenly find you have "got" a stroke and feel you can make it any time you want to—forevermore.

No doubt practice is good for you, healthy, good exercise, etc. But all that is nothing to a tennis player. You're there for just one thing: to master your strokes.

Forehand

Watch the ball. Keep watching it. By the end of the afternoon it looks slow no matter how hard your opponent hits it and it "grows" as big as a softball. The shots your opponent sends over to you are not difficult, it's just that you can't hit the ball properly all the time.

You find you hit too many in the net and you decide that's the most complete waste you've ever come across. So you make your first great improvement: You hit every ball over. You can scramble even the lowest one over if you're determined enough.

Some of your shots are going out. You've let the ball drop too low and then you lifted it too far. Use your feet more quickly, hit the ball from that comfortable waist height, and you will feel it's on its way over the net and in. Not always in, so you want more ball control. Long contact. Longer and longer contact, till you feel that unless you hit the ball yards over the net, it could not go out.

How high over the net should you be hitting the ball anyway? You had thought of tennis as a low, skimming-the-net sort of game—but now that you're playing it, it's not quite like that. You send a lot of balls here and there, and when you do finally manage to skim one over the net it lands short and you can see that your opponent plays it easily.

Here is a guide: Driving from baseline to baseline, you should clear the net by the length of a racket or more. (See Illus. 24.)

You find the singles court is not as wide as you had thought. Standing in the middle of it you can run to either side and reach almost any ball. Even so, when you run wide to one side and linger there, the next ball down the other sideline is well out of reach. You have discovered a well-used tennis tactic: when you have played from the side, return *at once* to the middle. Later this becomes instinctive.

Your hand is getting tired. You haven't been playing long, and in general you're as fresh as a daisy. Therefore, the trouble is that you have been gripping your racket tightly all the time. So take the racket back easily and firm up your grip as you swing forward. Relaxing this small but necessary amount, you notice your swing is smoother. Try to get more smoothness by making your swing travel at the same speed throughout, instead of jerking forward just before hitting the ball. You will notice that this smoothness improves your timing.

What was that again about timing? It was that players tend to be too early with their swing. So you should delay your forward swing a fraction, mentally. Do not make a drastic pause, like bringing your racket to a stop.

Timing and smoothness. Long contact. Sooner or later, you're going to feel comfortable.

Illus. 25. TIMING ERROR. Mostly you hit too early. The best proof of this occurs when you attempt a smash, and miss the ball altogether. No one ever smashes at the ball *after* it has gone by.

Try aiming. Send forehands straight to your opponent, to his forehand corner, and to his backhand. To aim straight you must get your body sideways to the net, the most correct position being with your hips in line with the intended direction of your stroke. Try to make all your forehands land about halfway between the service line and the backline. That is a fairly good "length," and good length or "deep" shots keep your opponent well back. And the farther back he is, the more time you will have to play his return.

Try some cross-court forehands, landing the ball near the service line. A lot will go out. Try rolling on some topspin. Come forward to the ball and feel yourself using your weight.

Chancing to be near the net, you try your hand at hitting a ball "on the full" or "on the fly"—and you send it all the way to the far fence. You felt powerful enough while doing this, but an instant later you realize that you had no constructive idea for this shot; no control. You recall that when you have seen good players play this shot—a volley—they seem to block the ball rather than swing at it. It is a completely different stroke, and we will come to it in the next chapter.

Similarly, when you again happen to be near the net, your opponent may lob the ball high above your head. Using your service action, you take a hearty swing at it. If you are normal, you miss the ball completely. *No* contact, let alone long contact. This is interesting. You have missed the ball altogether by hitting *too soon*. (See Illus. 25.) No one ever swings too late and misses a ball by hitting at it *after* it has gone by. Your short experience of being so early that you completely miss the ball reinforces your understanding of timing your forehand: namely, that you must delay your forward swing a fraction.

The best that can be said for fooling about at the net with strokes you haven't yet learned is that it is clean and wholesome. So back to the baseline you go. Back to your business.

Backhand

You know that your grip plays an important part in your backhand. Take your grip carefully and play a succession of backhand shots without changing back to your forehand grip after any of them.

Realize that your backhand grip is a strong grip and also that you would naturally throw rings backhanded. This saves you from feeling powerless and strange. Nevertheless, give your backhand every chance. Stand well inside the backline at first and play your backhands from there.

The early enemy of everyone's backhand is the net. When an experienced coach stands at the net and throws over a ball for a pupil to attempt his first-ever backhand, the coach has no illusions at all. He knows where the ball is going: right into the net.

Hit the Ball Farther in Front of You

To get your backhands over the net, you must be determined to meet the ball nearer the net than on your forehand (farther ahead of your front hip as you stand sideways to the net—in fact, a good 6 inches ahead of that hip). Aim to hit the ball well over the net—two racket-heights, almost 6 feet—because you are unlikely to hit your early backhands out.

You feel somewhat mortified. A moment ago, when you ended your forehand practice, you were making progress and becoming quite positive—and now you're back to novice stage, scratching about in frustration. Take courage. The path you are following is a well-worn one, trod by thousands before you —thousands who ended as good players with sound backhands.

Watch the ball. Turn well sideways to the net. Swing at one pace instead of jerking. Have confidence that your backhand grip has strength in it. Aim straight ahead, no angles. Long contact. *Over* the net. Again, and again . . . and yet again.

Smoothness and Timing

Your hand is getting tired. Relax your grip as you swing

back, and firm up as you swing forward. That feels better, and your swing becomes smoother.

What about timing? You haven't noticed it so much. Why?

Because you have already had some forehand timing experience and because backhand timing is easier anyway. The swing is shorter and is not looped, and your wrist is stronger.

Now your arm is getting tired, since you are hitting from the unaccustomed backhand side. Because you haven't had to change grip, you have probably been making the whole stroke using your right arm only. That is not necessary. Take your racket back with both hands: right hand on the handle in your usual backhand grip (Illus. 13); left-hand fingertips and ball of thumb on the racket's throat. When you reach the end of your backswing, pause—now part your arms: right arm forward to hit the ball, and left arm out behind you for balance and smoothness.

When you can comfortably hit your backhand smoothly over the net and straight ahead, where you are aiming, you can move farther back and practice more backhands from there. Please note that the idea is not to learn a stroke while standing at the back of the court. The emphasis is on learning to hit a stroke smoothly and comfortably, just as the experienced players do.

That's enough backhand for one session. *Finish your practice with some forehands* and feel like a tennis player again.

Next Session

It's tomorrow now—and you should have sufficient interest to want to practice every day in any playable weather, so that you will not feel your game has gone back between practices. At this, your second practice session, you recommence with more forehands, and then play a number of backhands of the same type as you finished with. There's some wind blowing. Rather than let that disturb you, make it assist. Convince yourself that you can hit more strongly against the wind and yet keep the ball in court, and that you can get speed with little effort when the wind is behind you.

Advance now to aiming your backhand to your opponent's backhand corner. You should aim straight for this corner, as you did when aiming straight down the middle. You do this by lining up your feet and hips. To hit to your opponent's backhand do not stand as though to hit straight ahead, and then pull the ball across your body. Pulling across the ball's line of flight is unsound and inaccurate. It may sometimes land your shot in the right place, but often this method of hitting pulls your shot too far across, and outside the sideline. Pulling across the ball is the cause of so many shots needlessly landing in the "alley," when you are playing a set.

Backhand Down the Line

If you base your backhand on lining up your feet and hips in the intended direction of your shot, you will have little trouble with your next effort, which is hitting your backhand to your opponent's forehand corner. This shot is the bugbear of those hundreds of players who learned their backhands wrongly, pulling them across court. Even when these players want to hit a backhand down the middle of the court, they vaguely aim it somewhat towards their opponent's forehand and then pull it round to the middle. When they want to hit to an opponent's forehand corner, or "down-the-line," they do not go so far as to aim the ball outside the court and pull it in. Instead, they play a different type of backhand altogether; they slice inside the ball (that is, hit the ball on the side nearest the body) and direct it to the off side, or down-the-line, in this way. All this leads to an inaccurate backhand, obviously. Also, the preparation for two different types of backhands warns the opponent in advance which corner the ball is coming to.

You should be sound from the beginning. Practice your backhand by hitting straight. Don't pull across the ball: use long contact.

When you have had enough undiluted backhand practice, play forehands and backhands as they come along. The natural way to carry a racket is with a forehand grip, and you already know how to change to your backhand grip. You use the ball of your left thumb and the tips of fingers and twist the throat a little, clockwise.

Service

The essentials of a champion's serve are his aiming with long contact and his smoothness. To this he adds speed, by means of a complete throwing action.

Clearly, you should practice aiming with long contact and with smoothness. So that "action" cannot possibly distract you, use your shoulder serve. So that you are certain to be smooth, begin by serving from as close to the net as you like and then move backwards little by little.

Serve only from the right side (left-handers from the left) into the court diagonally opposite you. Take advantage of this diagonal swing of the ball. It aids your feeling that you have attained that slight swerve in your shot. And this feeling, in turn, adds to your feeling of having long contact. It does not matter how slight this swerve is, the feeling should be there. The *feeling* counts, *not* the amount of swerve.

Fortunately, serving can be practiced without an opponent. You can go to the court early, when no one is about, or very late. Collect all the old balls you can, in fact as many as you can carry. The balls will be in varying condition, of course: some hard, some soft, some worn and some used only once. Do not fuss over trifles like these. Take them all and serve them all, from your right side to the court diagonally opposite you, then change ends and serve them all back again.

Be Smooth

If only you will not think you are too big or too old or too adult to begin from serving near the net, you can develop an easy serve by stages, one that you can have for the rest of your life. Please contrast that with the anxious and hard-working serves you sometimes see used by players who have played for many years. Many players regard their serving games almost as being a test of nerve and fortitude.

Fall into Your Routine

Wherever you stand, line up the toes of your shoes, bend your elbow sharply, cock your wrist by your shoulder, and advance the ball you are serving to between the ball of your thumb and your fingertips, throw it up, watch it, let it settle, and then hit it smoothly with aim and long contact and try to feel a trace of swerve. Only a trace, or I will be sorry I ever mentioned this swerve.

As your practice sessions take you through each different stage in building up your complete throwing-action serve—shoulder-serve—racket behind back—racket looped behind back—swing started from feet—and, finally, swing started from in front of waist—there is no reason why you should not start each new stage by serving from closer to the net than the baseline. You are practicing, remember, not playing a set. Do not take the slightest chance of developing an awkward service action. If you are a man, be smooth; if a girl, be graceful. Both will add to the power you will have later.

Serving *Over* the Net

By the time that you are regularly serving from the normal serving position behind the baseline, you will have had enough experience to know that the net is your enemy. It is a worse enemy to your serve than it is to your backhand, or to any low-bouncing ball, and in fact it is a worse enemy than even your opponent. Many players have not realized this and even after years of playing, they hit first serve after first serve uselessly into the net. So remember this advice: After you have hit two first serves in succession into the net, get your next first service *over*, at any speed.

Your service action is a downward one, giving the ball a downward tendency. So as soon as you cease concentrating on getting the ball over, it is likely to go into the net. The net is the great catcher.

Another cause of serving into the net is throwing the ball too low. Yet another is throwing it too far forward. Throwing it higher and a little farther back makes a lot of difference.

Sometimes the harder you try, the more certainly the ball goes in the net. The reason, unknown to you at the time, is that you are falling forward. Here is a certain cure: keep the toe of your back foot on the ground until your racket has hit the ball. This technique also shows you at once if you have been unknowingly throwing the ball too far forward.

Why Your Serve Sometimes Goes Out

All this has made it sound as though your serve goes only into the net and never out, and yet you know from your own practice experience that it often goes out. Naturally, you want to know why.

The answer is that you have not watched the ball well enough and so have not hit it with the center of your strings. You can aim with certainty only from the center of your racket face.

Please turn back and look at Illus. 1 again, seeing the racket as upright and about to hit the ball in a serve. If you hit the ball with the center of the racket, it goes where you aim. If you hit it just above the center of the racket, it goes a little lower. If you hit below the center of the racket, it seems to fly up in the air. The real reason for this flying-up effect is that your racket is still sloping somewhat backwards towards the fence behind you as you serve the ball. However, the practical way to look at it is to hit with the very center of your racket strings (or just above center) and never below it. Below-center is the danger area that makes your serve go high and out, even when you try to hit more softly for safety's sake.

Your Second Serve

Another thing to realize when you are practicing is that your second serve is a more important stroke than your first. You can miss your first serve and still win the point, but you can't do this with your second. Having a reliable second serve will make you a relaxed match-player later on. A player with a crashing first serve and an unsafe second ball may appear to be a giant in a practice set, but he is always likely to be timid in a match. Enjoy yourself as much as you like hitting your first serve hard, but do not neglect to practice your second. In a match you will need to get as many first serves in as possible, and practically every second ball you have to serve.

Practice Sets

As soon as you can manage to land a few serves into court from the backline, you will find that your opponent wants to play a set instead of giving you hits. You cannot very well refuse him, but you should concentrate on playing your forehand, backhand, and serve in the form you are practicing—and let the meaningless score take care of itself. Get your strokes first. Later you can scramble to win.

That is how I think your practice should—and will—be. It will not consist of hitting 50 forehands here, 50 forehands there, and another 50 somewhere else—repeated with the backhand. No one will be partner to this sort of practice, except perhaps some devoted parent. You will have to take care of your own practice, using the facts and guidelines you receive from this book and also the mental pictures you have stored up of experienced players. For learning strokes you can't beat having a coach, but even then you have to put your own mind into your practice and get your *own* long contact on the ball.

If you manage to take possession of a court only late in the afternoon, play until it is too dark to see. Dinner does nothing for your strokes.

8. YOUR OTHER STROKES

ONCE YOU CAN ATTACK with your forehand and feel solid with your backhand, and can aim your serve smoothly into court, you will have broken the back of stroke-making. Other strokes may necessitate your getting into position quicker or something like that, but as strokes in themselves they are easier to make.

Lob

When your opponent is at the net, lift the ball over his head. That is all the inventor of the first lob did—on the spur of the moment, without his ever having practiced it. Such a stroke—a lift—is easy to do.

Don't jump or hop, merely because you are hitting upwards. As you did with your drives, watch the ball, turn sideways to the net, and aim with long contact.

Always lob deeply. That is, try to make the ball land nearer your opponent's backline than his service line. Every tennis player has a natural tendency to lob short. You are used to stepping into your drives and using your weight, but in making a lob you may be standing still. This causes your lob to be short—unless you are aware of it.

Volley

The volley (hitting the ball before it bounces) adds dash to your game.

You want to maintain naturalness in volleying. Volleys generally have to be made swiftly, so naturalness is at a premium. There is little point to my providing photographs or diagrams which give no idea of the speed involved. You should get the picture live from a coach or by watching a competent volleyer in action. Then your volleying will be natural and instinctive—which is the only way for it to be quick enough.

To volley a ball, do not swing at it—punch it. If it comes at you fast, block it. Put your racket against the ball as naturally as you would put your hand there to catch it. Do not doubt your ability to play backhand volleys, because your backhand grip is strong for short shots like volleys.

The ideal and soundest of volleys are made with the same basic routine you use for drives: Watch the ball, turn sideways to the net, aim with long contact. However, often there is no time for all this, in which case the shot comes down to watching the ball (you are already continuously watching it, remember?) getting your weight going forward (even if you are square-on to the net), and blocking the ball over the net.

Similarly, when you have time you use your two different grips for forehand and backhand volleys. You will always have time for this when your opponent is trying to pass you with drives from the back of the court. But if he is also near the net, as you are, you may play a forehand volley and the next instant receive a backhand one. If so, volley the ball with whatever grip you happen to have on the handle. You may be able to aim to some degree, but you will have no thought of long contact.

High and Waist-high Volleys

High volleys, meaning shoulder-high and above, are easy. After due practice, which you must give to any stroke, you will find that you will miss them only through carelessness. This carelessness occurs in not watching the ball, not turning sideways, and not aiming with long contact. Of these three factors, the usual form of carelessness with high volleys is not bothering to turn sideways.

Waist-high volleys are probably the most natural shots you can make in tennis. Most people find them so. The reason why some few do not is that they can't get away from the ground-stroke technique of using a swinging stroke.

Low Volleys

Low volleys, meaning balls travelling below net height and particularly those near the ground, can be difficult. Girls doubt that they have enough strength in their wrists to play a very low one as a blocked shot; and so they swing at them—disastrously. Moreover, whether you are male or female, the easiest place to hit a very low volley is into the net.

When you play a very low volley, determine to lift it (or force it) over the net. This is merely mind over matter. A helpful point of technique is to let the frame of your racket hit the ground. The support from the court makes your wrist feel a lot stronger. Using a Continental grip (Illus. 12) also helps in lifting very low volleys over the net.

Not all very low volleys will come straight at your feet. So, by bending your knees swiftly and deeply you can get your waist down to the ball and play with your racket about parallel to the ground. This puts you back to your comfortable waist-high position again. It is the correct way to play any low volley and it is the way you will see champions play them.

To discuss the most difficult low volley of all, the one straight at your feet—please get your racket out. Playing this shot as a forehand, your racket will be perpendicular, which allows you little control. Also it will be in front of your legs, thus interfering with your bending your knees. Now regard the ball-on-your-shoelaces volley as a backhand. You will see that you can move your right hand over to the right side of your legs. This allows you to bend your knees, and you can then have your racket parallel to the ground to some degree instead of having it perpendicular with little control. Finally, your backhand grip is stronger. Volleying off your shoelaces need not be a matter of luck. Regard it as a backhand shot, and your chances will be a lot better.

Court Position and Reflex

As far as racket work is concerned, all volleys are easier than drives. Volleys, however, need good court position and quickness to back them up—far more than drives do.

For speed of reflex, many advanced volleyers adopt a grip halfway between forehand and backhand (again, similar to Illus. 12) and use it for volleys on either side.

Half-volley

This stroke is made just as the ball leaves the ground, like a drop-kick in football.

It is easy if you go into it; difficult if you hesitate. The secret in playing it is to half-volley the ball *at the instant it leaves the ground*, allowing it its least possible bounce.

You may have heard that you should never play a half-volley, that you should either go forward and volley or go back and play a groundstroke. This old adage is correct only when you have plenty of time. Otherwise it will land you in trouble. If you are short of time, the volley you attempt to make will be so low that the ball will hit the frame of your racket near the ground. Similarly your retreating would-be groundstroke will be difficult and probably mis-hit. If you have no time at all, you will have to play a half-volley anyway. And you have a better chance with a straightforward half-volley than with any kind of messed-up volley or groundstroke.

As with very low volleys, bend your knees quickly and deeply (squat down) and try to play with your racket parallel to the ground as much as possible. Again, little or no backswing is required. However, do not punch the ball as in a volley. Instead, push your racket through after a half-volley, in long contact and follow-through.

This is the technique, but the whole basis is to take the ball *close* to the ground. Go for it as a stroke with every chance of success. Don't hesitate. But don't hit it hard. It is mainly a touch shot.

Smash

The smash, or overhead stroke, is the "Big Gun" of tennis because it can be hit harder and bounced higher than any other stroke. However, you should know from the start that the main thing you require of your smash is solidity. If you go up to the net intending to volley, you must have a solid overhead in reserve. Otherwise you are like a house without a roof, having no protection against rain, or lobs.

Smash versus Serve

Some players regard a smash as more difficult than a service because the ball needs more timing. Others say that the timing is only a matter of waiting longer for the ball, and that a smash is far easier than a serve because you play from closer to the net and you have the whole of your opponent's court to hit it into. I take the latter view, wholeheartedly.

A player's smash always looks like his service, and this has given rise to the incorrect idea that your smashing action should be identical with your service action. This is wrong and will cause unnecessary complication and uncertainty with your overhead if you follow it.

You should smash with your shoulder-serve action. Do not call into action all the service swing you use to propel an almost stationary ball all the way from behind the backline. To do so is both unnecessary and dangerous.

Illus. 26. SETTING YOURSELF FOR A SMASH. With no unnecessary action you have only to time the ball, hit the center of your strings (or a little above center), and send the ball *over* the net. A large amount of court is waiting to receive it.

Smashing Technique

Please look at Illus. 26. When a lob comes to you, put your left hand up in line with it. This sets and keeps you sideways to the net. Cock your racket near your right shoulder, your elbow well bent. Wait. Wait. Wait: the ball is not yet in hitting range. When it is, rise to meet it. This makes your timing more positive than waiting longer on the ground and feeling that the ball is going to fall on top of you. Hit the ball with the center of your strings (*never* below center) and aim it *over* the net (because at least 7 out of every 10 missed smashes go down into the net).

Use this simple action and be determined to hit with the center of your strings. All you have to practice is your timing. You will be standing halfway in court and you have the whole opposite court to play into.

Smash solidly. Lash out for pure enjoyment only when the lob is short.

Slice, Cut, Chop, Chip

Whatever these terms may put you in mind of, they are tennis strokes.

All are regarded as belonging to the "underspin family." Admittedly, if you slice downwards against the outside of a high ball, most of the spin you impart will be sidespin. However, even with this there is a little underspin. Remember that no strokes from slice to chip have any topspin and none are flat. All carry underspin.

Besides slicing outside the ball, you can slice under it; also partially under and inside it, as displayed in Illus. 16 and 17. When these strokes are made with a reasonably long action, they are called "slices." The same strokes made with a short action are called "cuts." A heavily cut stroke is called a "chop." When a player advances swiftly to the ball (such as to his opponent's second serve) and cuts it and moves into the net after it, all in one motion, the term "chip-approach" is mostly used.

All these shots are easily made (including the slice) because they do not involve a long swing. They are usually stronger on the backhand, where the stronger grip makes up for the lack of swing. On either side they are often used as a handy sort of shot when little time is available. All have a degree of long contact, and so all are safe. All hang in the air somewhat, and so are easy to volley. All are mostly unsuitable as passing shots against an opponent at the net.

The chop has a low bounce. On a wet court it slithers. Being heavily cut, however, it is the easiest of the underspin strokes to mis-hit.

All four are convenience or opportunity strokes or safety measures. As a foundation for your ground-game they are no substitute for forehand and backhand drives.

Drop-Shots

Drop-shots are used to drop the ball short over the net with little speed, stranding your opponent at the back of the court.

You should not expect to use them much, but if you have been driving deeply and your opponent has decided to stay well back to handle your drives, he may give you the chance to drop-shot him now and then. Choose a short ball of his to do this, because attempted drop-shots played from well back are seldom successful. Your opponent has more time to reach them, and also you are likely to land too many of them in the net.

Drop-shots demand touch. Therefore you should feel that you are holding the racket handle in your fingers. Use underspin, never overspin. In addition to the delicate, clinging-to-the-strings feeling that softly played under-and-inside spin can give, the ball will bounce lower.

Play your first drop-shots when your opponent is near the

back fence and you are near the net. Then you will see the shot can be a winner without being almost perfect.

All your strokes have now been described, from detailed advice about your invaluable forehand to brief remarks about the comparatively little-used drop-shot. (Left-handed strokes have their own characteristics, and we shall look at them in Chapter 11.)

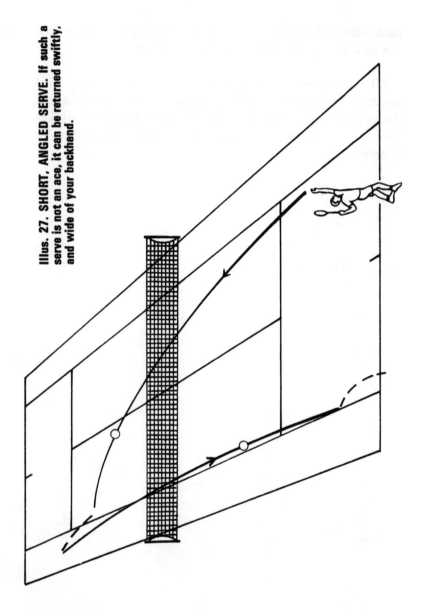

Illus. 27. SHORT, ANGLED SERVE. If such a serve is not an ace, it can be returned swiftly, and wide of your backhand.

9. SINGLES

YOU HAVE NOW LEARNED the mechanics of the game: watching the ball and controlling it, all your grips, the basic strokes, and the other shots that round out your game. The next thing to do is to apply them in singles-play.

Baseline Game

Your early sets should be played from the baseline. This type of game is the simplest and gives you the most time to play your shots. Its basis is aiming your three main shots—service, forehand, and backhand—with long contact and into court.

Let's assume you are about to play a serious set of singles. Your object is no longer to practice your strokes, but to gain experience in how to win.

You normally begin with a warm-up of less than 5 minutes. Don't waste this time merely loosening up or trying to get warm, expecting to concentrate on your strokes when the set starts. Concentrate at once—on watching the ball, aiming straight down the court with long contact, and trying to groove your strokes smoothly. Play forehands and backhands and, when it is nearly time to start, try half a dozen serves from each side of the center mark. Don't prolong the warm-up. You should want to get on to the experience of trying to win a set.

If you win the toss, you should choose to serve. More service

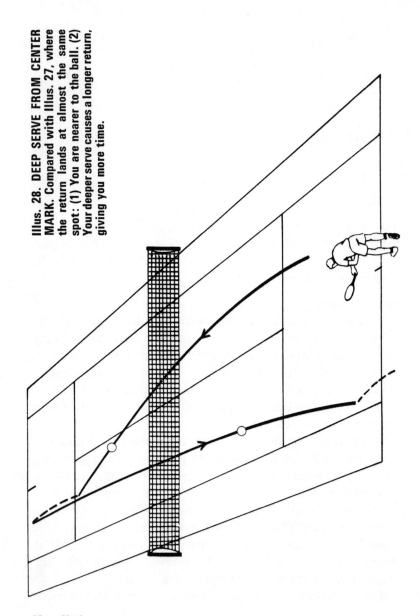

Illus. 28. DEEP SERVE FROM CENTER MARK. Compared with Illus. 27, where the return lands at almost the same spot: (1) You are nearer to the ball. (2) Your deeper serve causes a longer return, giving you more time.

games are won than lost, and it is far better to be a game ahead and trying to break your opponent's serve than to be a game down and trying to hold your own serve. It's never too early to start winning, so if you win the toss be positive and serve first.

Serving from the Right Side

Stand close to the center mark. This divides the two sides of the court which you have to cover on return about equally. Also, you expose your backhand side to minimum attack this way. As a general rule, do not serve from a point wide of the center mark, hoping for an angled ace. If your serve is not an ace, your opponent can return it right down the line, wide of your backhand. (See Illus. 27.)

Take time to line up the toes of your shoes and don't hurry, but do not delay either. Always be ready to get on with the game, because this helps to make you a quicker and more aggressive player. Aim your serve with long contact, hit with the center of your strings, and send the ball over the net. If a serve like that misses, it is at least what is called a "good sighter" for the second.

Unless a serve is an angled ace, depth is normally better to strive for than angle. (See Illus. 28.)

If your opponent is a left-hander, his backhand is easy to attack when you are serving from the right side. Again, it is better to serve deeply (to the corner of his right court) than to angle the ball shorter.

Angle and Depth

With any stroke, service or any other, if you play an angle you open up more of your own court to your opponent's return. This does not mean that you must avoid using angles completely and always hit your shots straight down the middle. You can aim for your opponent's backhand, you can change to his forehand if you feel that his backhand is having too much

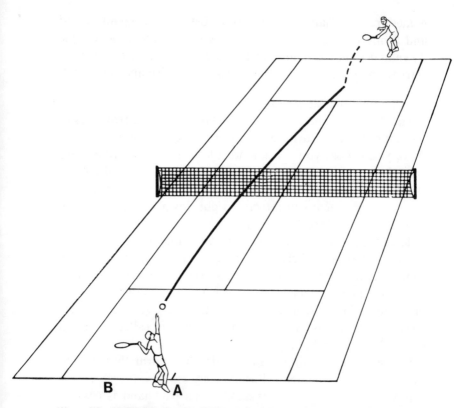

Illus. 29. SERVING FROM THE LEFT SIDE, TO A LEFT-HANDER. The server stands close to the center mark at "A" and attempts a center line serve, but serves a fault. He feels his second serve may be a double fault if he tries to land it close to the center line, and decides to get it safely into court instead. To avoid leaving his own backhand side wide open to an attack made against his weaker second serve, he can move wider out to "B" to serve his second ball.

practice and is getting solid, and you can try to put the ball out of his reach for a clean winner—or nearly out of reach so that his shot will be weak. You may also place your shots on one side and then the other, to make your opponent run for all his shots instead of letting him set himself comfortably to make them.

You will often use angles, but the fact remains that if your opponent can easily reach the ball, then the wider the angle you have played, the more of your court you will have uncovered and the easier it is for your opponent to return a winner because of your angled shot.

Depth is always safe, provided you use long contact to keep the ball in court. Depth makes your opponent hit the ball from farther back, at his end of the court. And this gives you more time to play his return shot.

Left-side Service

Most players when serving from the left side prefer to stand as much as 2 yards wide of the center mark. From there you will find it easier to serve to an opponent's backhand. You will leave more court open, but you will be covering this with your forehand. And in any case few opponents have a dangerous down-the-line backhand.

When serving to a left-hander, you may like to stand near the center for your first serve, to try to swerve the ball down the center line to his backhand. If your first serve misses, you may not care to risk leaving so much of your backhand side open, so you can move wider out and serve your second ball from there. (See Illus. 29.)

If a right-handed opponent has a poor backhand you can attack it constantly by serving from wide on the left side. If his backhand is reasonably sound, it is better to serve deeply than to angle the ball short to his backhand.

Serving for Depth to Either Side

To serve with depth, aim just short of the service line. Your serve, having a downward tendency, will land a little shorter than your aim, if you have hit either with the center of your strings or just above center. Serving for depth assists you in always serving *over* the net. A serve does not have to land within inches of the service line to be deep. Two feet inside is still deep, so do not demand too much of yourself.

Receiving Service

As a general guide: in the right court stand just behind the backline and about 2 feet inside the singles sideline; in the left court stand slightly behind the corner made by the backline and sideline. However, your receiving position is determined mainly by the server. If he stands wide of the center mark to serve an angle, you move wider to cover it. If his serve is slow, you stand inside the backline to receive it.

You may choose where you will return the ball, but most service-returns are directed to the server's backhand. If you are able to return the ball deeply to any part of the court, you will have nullified the advantage that the server has to begin with and you gain an even chance to win the point. It is easier said than done (to return the ball deeply, that is), but that is all it takes.

Rallying

A rally is any exchange of strokes.

Keeping to your basic routine of watching the ball, turning sideways, trying to take most balls at waist height and aiming with long contact, you should play mostly to your opponent's weaker side (usually his backhand). However, you can (1) vary your direction, (2) try to surprise him with an angle, (3) catch him off balance, (4) hit a clean winner, (5) keep him running, (6) wear him down, or (7) play a drop-shot if he gives you a short ball and stays well back himself. With all these variations open to you, you can see that the game can scarcely be dull, even though it is confined to baseline.

Position

Although you may have remembered the rule to return at once to the middle of the court after you have been forced wide, your footwork will be dreadfully slow at first. When you were practicing your strokes you tended to remain where you were after you had hit the ball. In fact, sometimes you may have remained halfway up the court. This won't do in a set. You have to hit the ball properly and then move at once to wherever you think you will be best positioned. Do not hang about in "no-man's land," the area between the back and service lines. Try to keep behind the baseline. You can move forward far quicker than backward. A rule of thumb is that you can take three steps forward in the time you can take one back.

Playing your first few sets, you may find yourself in the wrong position as early as immediately after your serve. Probably you swing your right leg over the line as you serve and step into court: most players do. If you wander one more step with your left foot, you will be standing well inside the baseline: in no-man's land. If your opponent plays a deep return, such as the player is doing in Illus. 27 or even his shot in Illus. 28, the ball will be behind you—and from this position you will almost certainly lose the point.

When you serve and swing your right leg over, your right foot meets the ground; it should then immediately return to parallel your left foot which is behind the backline, before your serve has bounced. You will then be in balance and also in good position.

Making Time for Yourself

No matter how fleet of foot you become, when you are forced wide you should not hit a fast return unless you are going for a winner or near-winner. The faster your shot reaches your opponent, the less time you will have to return to cover the open court you have left behind. When forced wide by a good shot, you should lob the ball back, high and deep, giving yourself plenty of time to return to the middle of your court and behind the backline.

What You Have Learned

The set you were trying to win comes to an end. It doesn't matter two straws if you won or lost. What matters is that you have learned something about winning. Here are four things I think you will have learned:

• Your strokes were not as reliable as you had imagined, and they need more practice.

• You were as slow as a cart horse.

• Position on the court seems to count about as much as strokes, when you play a set.

• You will never win a set against an equal opponent without trying hard to win; and a stroke is really a combination of correct mechanics and the will you put behind it.

All-Court Tennis

This term applies to singles-play when you vary your baseline-game with net attacks.

Whenever you feel you have time to advance to the net, to pause, and to be able to volley or smash your opponent's return, do just that. Going up to the net when you have little chance of being able to put your racket on the ball is mis-judgment rather than all-court tennis.

You must play an all-court game whenever you play someone whose deep driving is better than yours. You will almost certainly lose, otherwise. Your volley is the answer to his deep drives. Deep drives clear the net by a racket length or more and are easy to volley. Your opponent will need to change his game—and he may not be able to.

You do not have to wait to see if any opponent is better from the baseline than you are. If you can volley well, you should always make use of this shot and play an all-court game.

Net Position

A point is easier to win from near the net than from the baseline. Many an opponent will give you a convincing demonstration of this. Learning from this, you will soon decide to go to the net and play your own share of the game from there.

Any discussion on net play assumes that you are capable of covering the net to a reasonable degree. A very young and small player will have to forgo the net for a few years. To cover a lob he would need to stand so far back that most of his volleys would be low ones, even half-volleys—and his wrist may not be equal to the strain.

When to Go to the Net

Go to the net whenever you have given your opponent such a difficult shot that his reply will be weak. Go in whenever you have landed the ball behind him. Try going in when you hit a good first serve to his backhand in the left court; you are likely to be able to volley his return, because few players have a good down-the-line backhand to use as a passing shot. Go in sometimes as a surprise.

Do not go in on your second serve or on any other short ball you play to your opponent.

Note what sort of shots your opponent comes in on, and wins by. This is a perfect example of learning from your defeats.

How to Take the Net

How you go in to the net is by means of an approach shot. I mentioned three examples a moment ago: a difficult shot, a shot behind your opponent, and a first serve to his backhand in the left court. You should hit all these with the intention of following them smoothly to the net, where you expect to pause, then volley. You should not hit a shot, stand and look at it, decide it has been a good one, and belatedly *rush* to the net. The delay will mean you are still moving forward after your opponent has hit the ball. When moving forward you cannot reach nearly as far to either side as when you are stationary. This is important enough to repeat: Plan to approach the net on your shot as you make it (you need not follow in if it goes wrong), approach smoothly, pause—and you are covering the net.

Where to Stand

How close to the net should you be? The first volley after your approach will necessarily be from farther back, but after that you can close to 3 yards from the net. If you are closer you will give yourself too little time to make your volley, let alone cover the ball if it is driven wide of you or lobbed. If a soft-hit ball is coming to you, of course you move in as close to the net as you can to hit it. Be careful not to touch the net and thus lose the point.

Do not be misled by the close net position often used by professionals. They have very fast reflexes and also can cover lobs that would be out of reach for an average player.

As you play the net game yourself, you will appreciate that the figure of approximately 3 yards is the merest guide. Circumstances will vary it. You may be tall or short, fast or slow, a good low volleyer or a poor one. Your opponent is an influencing factor, too. His usual shot may be a cross-court drive, against which—to limit his angle—you should be as reasonably close to the net as possible. In contrast, he may rely mostly on lobbing, and you will have to position yourself far enough back to prevent these lobs from being out of your reach. It is here you will realize that your overhead should be a solid shot rather than an occasional crash against a weak lob.

Court Surface

When two champions play each other, the type of surface makes a big difference in the amount of net attack and volleying that each uses. When the game is being played on grass, a service bounces faster and lower and the receiver has less chance of making a passing shot than he has on clay, where the ball bounces slower and higher. You hear much of "grass-court players" and "clay-court players." So much distinction is made that you could be forgiven for thinking that on grass you should be at the net all the time—and on clay, never.

You should not let this influence your own game in the slightest. If you hit a short ball on grass, don't go in. If you land a ball behind your opponent on clay, you should be at the net. If you can play good all-court tennis on one surface, you can play it on another. I will go further and say that if you can beat an opponent on a clay court you can beat him on a grass one too, if you put your mind to it instead of indulging in self-pity.

Opposing an All-Court Player

You should try to keep your own shots deep, to restrict his chances of making approach-shots and following them to the net. When he has the net position, try to pass him straight down the sideline. Direct your forehand drive past his backhand volley, or aim your backhand past his forehand volley. Hitting straight down the line usually means you are aiming at the most open target. If you feel he is expecting such a shot and is going to move to cover it in the same instant that you are committed to this shot, you should try to angle past him across his body by means of a topspin drive. If you feel he is about to crowd in closer to the net to block off your intended angle, you should lob. Remember to hit your lobs hard enough, or they are certain to be short. Whenever possible, lob over your opponent's backhand side where he cannot reach as high. Even if you are a

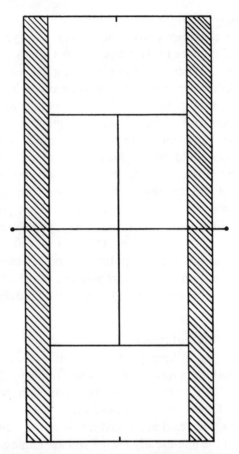

Illus. 30. DEPTH BEFORE ANGLE IN SINGLES.

Length:	26 yards
Net to Service Line:	7 yards
Service Line to Baseline:	6 yards
Width:	9 yards

baseline player, come to the net now and then, to prevent your opponent's "owning" the net position.

Serve-and-Volley Game

This means coming to the net to volley after every serve, first and second. The server serves, advances to about the *T* intersection of the service line and center line, pauses a second, volleys deeply, and then moves closer in for a second volley— which he hopes will decide the point for him.

Clearly you can play a serve-and-volley game only when both your first and second serves are good enough to be sound approach-shots. Otherwise you will be merely going to the net on a short ball, and that is *asking* to be passed.

If you want to play a serve-and-volley type of game, you will be wise to confine it, for some time, to following in to the net on first serves only. One good aspect of this is that it makes you determined to get a lot of first balls into play, instead of wasting them.

Depth before Angle

Depth of shot counts heavily in singles. You may have thought it important only in a baseline-game and that once volleying comes in, angles are better. You have seen champions end many points with sharply angled volleys well out of the reach of their luckless opponents.

"Well out of reach" is exactly the point. Champions do not play an angled volley unless this shot is going to win the point outright, or almost outright. Far more often they rely on depth. Note that when we were discussing the serve-and-volley game a moment ago, the keynote of the server's first volley was depth.

The importance of depth will become clearer to you when you realize how long and narrow a singles court really is. You should regard the singles court as being 26 yards by 9 yards, a ratio of nearly 3 to 1—and that "one" a mere 9 yards! To have a clear mental picture of the singles court you play on, see Illus. 30 (drawn lengthwise as the ball travels). It leaves little doubt that depth of shot should be predominant in your play.

10. DOUBLES

YOU HAVE PROBABLY SEEN a championship doubles match played. If you have not, let me briefly describe how I think one would appear to you.

Your first impression would be of all four players being at the net, exchanging rapid-fire volleys. One player eventually gives ground and has either to play the ball high or leave an opening, and you see the point decided by a final winning volley.

When you became more accustomed to the game, you would be able to follow how each of the four players gained his place at the net. You would notice that the server's and receiver's partners had already stationed themselves at the net, diagonally opposite each other, before the server served to the receiver. After the serve, the server followed in after the ball, making three players at the net. If the receiver made an attacking service return, he too followed in and then all four players were at the net.

Eventually you will play doubles in the same pattern. Let us see how you work up to it.

One Up and Three Back

Doubles takes this form when the players cannot volley well and so are not net-conscious. Only the server's partner is at

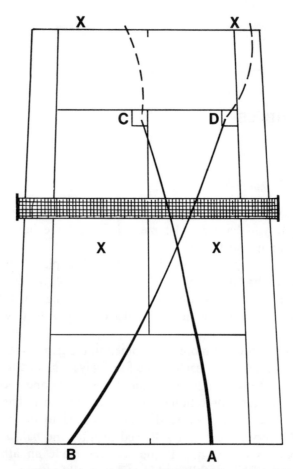

Illus. 31. BASIC DOUBLES SERVICES. Right side, A: Serve from about halfway between the center mark and sideline, because you have a wider area of court than in singles. You now have to cover the doubles sideline. Left side, B: Serve from somewhat wider than you do from the right side. This protects your backhand more, and gives your serve a better angle towards your opponent's backhand. Both sides: Aim for the imaginary deep backhand squares C and D. These services give a receiver less chance of attacking than any others do. Being deep, they also give your net partner more time to make an interception.

the net, to put away an easy ball that may come his way. In more aggressive tennis of a higher standard, this net player tries to intercept the ball at every opportunity. Having served, the server remains at the baseline, and so do the receiver and his partner. The server tries to win the point himself with his drives, or else tries to force either of his opponents into making a shot that his net-partner can volley for a winner. The receiving side tries to outplay the server or pass the net-man down his sideline.

One Up on Each Side

As each partner receives service, his partner stands at the net (or on the service line, and closes into the net if the service return is a good shot). Thus both sides have a man at the net, and both sides are looking for a kill. The game can reach a reasonably high standard, as there is ample opportunity for a variety of strokes to be used. Most improving doubles-pairs play in this formation for some time, until their play becomes sufficiently strong for them to progress beyond it. Meanwhile, assuming this will be the type of doubles that you, in turn, will play for a time, let us look at it in some detail.

Serving in doubles, you should serve from about halfway between the center mark and the doubles sideline, because you have a wider court to protect. (See Illus. 31 for more detail.)

As always, depth is the most important factor, but you should confidently try a number of variations. From the right side, you should now and again swerve the ball wide of the receiver's forehand. He may not be able to return it out of your net partner's reach. Or, serve it down the center line. Again, he may have difficulty in directing his return away from your net man. From the left side you should usually serve to the backhand side, but you can now and then serve down the center line and try to surprise your opponent. Illus. 31, combining depth with an attack on your opponents' backhands, shows

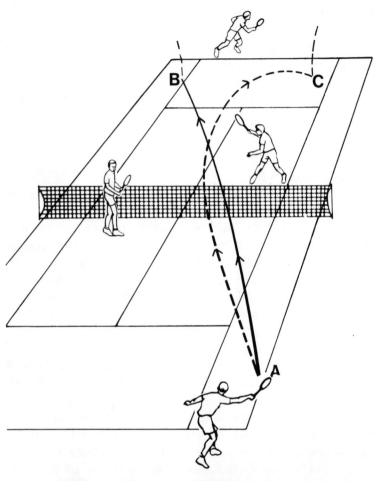

Illus. 32. SERVER PLAYING FROM THE BASELINE. You serve (not shown) and the receiver returns the ball to you (not shown). You hit his return at point A. You usually exchange drives with him, such as AB, or lob the ball over his partner's head, AC. Occasionally you can make a passing shot down the receiving net man's sideline. However, more often he tries to tempt you to try this.

serves from the right and left sides that you should try to make your two stock serves.

If your serve is returned to you, exchange drives with your opponent or vary things by lobbing well over his net partner's head and making the receiver cross over and play the ball from well back. Your net partner may be able to intercept his shot. (See Illus. 32.)

Net Man

When you are the net man do not stand very close to the sideline or very close to the net. You will put yourself out of the game. Except for guarding your sideline like an immovable sentinel, you will be of no help to your partner. It will then become a game of two against one. When the two prevail you may say to yourself that your partner lost his serve, but in truth you did almost nothing to help him win it.

As a guide, stand about 3 yards from the net. Stretch out your arm and racket to reach the sideline and then stand a little closer to the middle than that. This is only a guide, so do not let it restrict you. Try standing in different positions.

When the receiver's partner is standing at the net, the court behind him is wide open for a winning shot, if you can reach one of the receiver's returns and volley it there. Playing in one set you may reap a harvest of winning volleys, making you decide you should stand closer and closer to the middle. In the next set another pair may teach you a swift lesson by driving ball after ball down your sideline, where your partner cannot possibly cover you. You should learn for yourself where to stand at the net. In general, if your partner serves short you will have little chance to intercept and volley.

In good time you will learn how to move slightly toward the middle just as the receiver is about to hit the ball, without leaving your sideline dangerously open. Meanwhile, you are sure to find it tempting (and often successful) to move toward

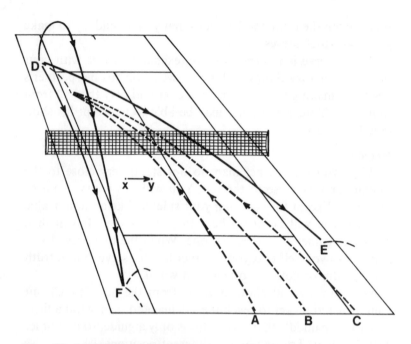

Illus. 33. RETURNS OF SERVICE

A-D-E: Server serves from near center mark A, to your forehand D.
You return a short cross-court topspin shot to E, wide of his position.
B-D-F: Server serves from B, halfway between center mark and sideline,
again to your forehand at D. Net man intends to intercept your return and
moves from x to y. You play a passing shot down the sideline to F.
C-D-F: Server serves from C, wide, again to your forehand D. You lob
over net man to F.

the middle when your partner has served wide. However, there is a balancing factor. The wider your partner serves, the more opening there is for a receiver to drive down your sideline. Here is an often-ignored rule: Move to the same side of the court as the ball.

Rules are made to be broken, of course. You should judge where to stand and how much you should move to intercept, and how often you can do so, by the type of strokes the receiver opposite you plays. A book can merely make you aware of such things. Only on the court do you learn how to apply them for yourself. But this advice stands: Intercept and make winning volleys as often as the receiver allows you to.

Receiving

You are playing in the right court. Here are various situations that could occur:

ONE. The server stands near the center mark and unwisely serves wide to your forehand. Following the old saying, "A good angle deserves a better one," you drive short across court with topspin. Your shot could be a winner, with the ball bouncing into the side fence before the server is even near it.

TWO. The server stands halfway between center mark and sideline and again serves wide to your forehand. The net man moves to intercept too early. You drive past him down his sideline. I have marked up another winner for you, but you will have had to work for it. The net is 6 inches higher at sideline than center, so there you always have to make extra sure your shot clears it—safely. Sideline attempts that strike the tape are often the result of non-awareness of the net's being higher there, rather than being bad luck. Second, many sideline shots pass the net man and then pass over the backline as well. So you must· drive over the net with either topspin or long contact, and aim for a spot inside the court.

THREE. The server stands wide out near the sideline and serves

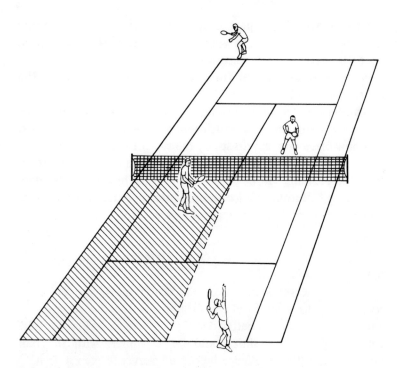

Illus. 34. NET MAN'S COURT COVERAGE. When the server follows his serve to the net, his net partner has to cover the whole of the shaded area—against center and sideline drives and against lobs.

to your forehand. You lob the ball over his partner's head and give the server a long backhand chase. (See Illus. 33 for these three examples.)

FOUR. The server again stands about halfway out (which covers his sideline, but without exaggeration this time) and serves the ball deep and to your forehand. He is improving. You should drive back to him with long contact as deeply as you can, and then you and your net partner await developments.

FIVE. The server serves from the same covering position (about halfway between center mark and sideline) deeply to your backhand. You manage to play the ball back to him, being rather relieved that it got past his net partner without being intercepted. Probably you felt somewhat lucky, because you had to play the serve from well back, and because your backhand to the offside is not strong when you are short of time to turn well sideways and aim it—and with a serve you often don't get much time. Learning from an opponent, you've found out what type of serve you don't much care for. Serve it yourself when it's your turn again.

Take off a minute now from reading this book and get out a pencil and paper. Draw some situations that could occur if you were receiving in the left court. Try them later on the court. Trying your own theories in practice is fascinating.

Sophisticated Doubles

This type of game, to be successful, demands a high standard of strokes and court position. You may not be playing it for a while, but here is an outline.

SERVING. You follow every service to the net, where you and your partner must then form an almost impenetrable barrier. He must cover all lobs attempted over his head (see Illus. 34 for the extent of his cover) and you must cover lobs over your head.

RECEIVING. Again your aim is to form a barrier with your partner, as you did when serving. The server allows you to do this if he does not follow his serve to the net. For example: he serves, you return and come to the net beside your partner. The advantage now belongs to your side instead of to the serving side—if both you and your partner can volley and smash well and are quick enough not to be lobbed over or caught by shots down near your feet. You can see that you need to have a fair degree of skill.

In championship doubles we have already seen that both pairs are completely net-conscious. The server comes in and forms a barrier with his partner. It is the receiver who has the hardest task of all. Against a good serve he tries to make his return of service so difficult for the serving pair's net barrier that he himself can afford to follow in after his shot. *That* is where the topmost skill comes in.

Clearly, you should play your one-up one-back doubles formation for a time. Later, try forming a net barrier with your partner (when serving or receiving) whenever you hit a strong serve or groundstroke. Build up to sophisticated doubles by trial and error, step by step. It may seem a long way off as you read this book, but if you have enough interest and determination it is the type of doubles you are sure to play one day.

11. LEFT-HANDERS

LEFT-HANDERS ARE NOT MADE differently from right-handers. Since there is no built-in disadvantage in your being left-handed, you should play tennis with whichever hand is naturally stronger and more deft. In practice, if you throw a ball left-handed, you should play tennis left-handed. A few natural left-handers play tennis right-handed. Even if they are good players, in every case they are handicapped to some extent, particularly with serve, overhead, and forehand.

Although you left-handers are not built differently from a right-hander, in tennis you develop different strokes. Left-handers who have learned tennis without guidance tend greatly to develop lopsided groundstrokes—strong forehand and weak backhand.

The Reasons Why

The reasons are not hard to find. Four people go onto a court for a game of tennis, and the left-hander always plays in the left court so that he and his partner can return most of the serves with their forehands. In fact, in any one set a left-hander plays more forehands than his right-handed partner. The opponents' serves do not swerve away from his forehand, so he can safely stand a little nearer the center to receive service, and thus play more forehands. He tends to become a specialist in forehand service returns. He uses a forehand grip that is

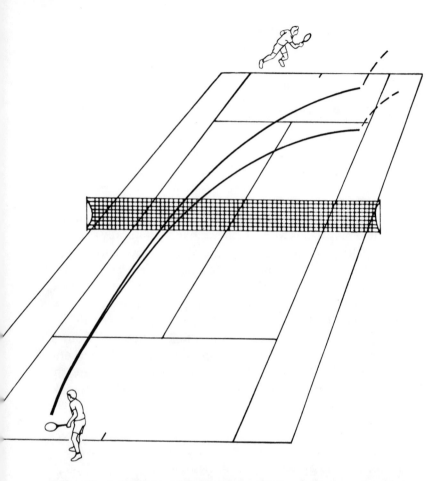

Illus. 35. A TYPICAL LEFT-HANDER'S TWO FAVORITE SHOTS. Often learning to play tennis from the left doubles court, many left-handers develop a wonderfully good topspin cross-court forehand drive. It plagues a right-hander, in singles or doubles.

suitable for short high balls, like serves, and does not worry much about his backhand. The grip he develops is shown in Illus. 11, and often his hand is even farther behind the handle. Such grips demand a large change for an adequate backhand grip to be taken, but the typical left-hander we are talking about is not much concerned with his backhand. I have warned left-handers of this pitfall as early as Chapter 3, on Grips.

Sometimes a serve reaches the protected backhand of the left-hander playing doubles in the left court. He hits it in his most natural direction, and it goes straight to the opposing net man, who volleys it away. To avoid the net man on future occasions he tries to steer his backhand away to the off side by raising his elbow and cutting inside the ball. He does this rather than make the large change he needs to make for an adequate backhand grip that will allow him to drive strongly.

In Singles, Too

When this type of left-hander plays singles his weak backhand is more exposed, but he still manages to play more forehands than his right-handed opponent. He pulls his left-handed forehand across court to his opponent's backhand. Most right-handers prefer making a cross-court backhand and are not very strong when hitting down-the-line, and so the left-hander again reaps his forehand harvest. (See Illus. 35.)

As the left-hander improves and plays against strong singles opponents, his weak backhand is too great a burden to bear. That is the reason why so few left-handers have won the world's major singles crowns. It took Rod Laver, carefully coached from youth to develop a balanced strength between forehand and backhand, to show left-handers the path they should follow. In this book, I have tried to show right-handers and left-handers alike the importance of having an adequate backhand grip, of turning sideways to the net, and of aiming straight with long contact.

Smash and Service

Here again an untutored left-hander develops noticeable characteristics. Although he pulls his forehand across court, he nearly always smashes away to his off side, that is, towards his right-handed opponent's forehand. He likes to serve this way too, instead of using a swerving slice service. Thus many left-handers waste their natural opportunity of having as their stock ball a fast and swinging service from the left side, going wide of the backhand of a right-hander receiving in the left court. See Illus. 35 again, and this time picture a series of swinging left-handed serves to the service box sideline—landing anywhere from deep in the corner of the box to halfway up the sideline and heading for the side fence. A left-hander can have a deadly service.

The left-hander's habit of serving to his off side, and hence of smashing in that direction too, is traceable to his having learned to serve from the same side as everyone else, namely, the right side of the court. It was the natural thing to do. A game starts from that side. That is where the tiny seed was planted. When speaking of service, I made a strong point of left-handers learning from the left side.

Spin

It is because left-handers seem to develop more spin and swerve than right-handers that some people have wondered if their wrists were not differently made. Left-handers probably do develop more spin since more of them specialize in it. They know that left-handed spin upsets many right-handers. Even if left-handed spin is not greater, it always appears so, because it is not in the usual direction. Left-handers also tend to use topspin rather than long contact as their basis of ball control.

Volleys

A left-hander's opponents say his volleying is unpredictable, while his doubles partner may complain that it is erratic.

Probably both are right. The left-hander's volley is a direct descendant of his service return, namely, a longer than normal forehand stroke and a short and square-to-the-net backhand. Unpredictable and erratic results are likely.

WHAT TO DO ABOUT IT

If you have begun your tennis with this book, or by taking lessons from a coach, you are already a balanced left-hander. You have now been made fully aware of what it all means.

However, it is likely that you have already played enough tennis without guidance to have settled into some or all of the left-handed characteristics I have described. As some of them amount to weaknesses, you will want to know what to do about them. Let's run through your strokes.

Smash

Leave it alone. If your first smash goes in, you usually win the point in any case. Also, most players, including right-handers, have a preferred direction for their smash. A discerning opponent soon detects which side of the court his opponent, left- or right-handed, likes to smash to. However, if he lobs short, this knowledge does him little good.

Serve

You can practice a sliced serve. From the left side, stand at least halfway between the center mark and the sideline, and swerve your serve over to the opposing sideline. From the right side, stand close to the center mark and swerve your serve down the center line. Take great care to do this gently for a time. Hitting at full speed too early with a new service action can cause long-term shoulder trouble.

Volleys

Now that you know, keep your forehand volley shorter, and turn sideways to the net for your backhand. Try to be very quick and change grip farther round for your backhand. The new feeling of strength in your backhand grip should be an incentive to make this larger change.

Backhand

In practice sets, tell your partner it is a good opportunity for you both to practice your backhands, and then head for the right court. From there you will have plenty of cross-court backhand play. You will also probably delight in the strength that comes from using an adequate backhand grip.

Forehand

Leave it. If you feel you hit the ball hardest and safest with a topspin action rather than with a straighter stroke, stay that way. Do not inhibit your best shot. Do not monkey about with as tricky a thing as a left-hander's highly individual way of hitting his own forehand. If you do, in later years you are likely to tell your friends that you had a good forehand once, until you read a book.

Large Change from Forehand to Backhand

This will remain your difficulty. Be as quick as you can. Practice using your fingertips and the ball of your right thumb on the throat of your racket to change grip.

Don't change anything in your game you don't need to change, whether you conform to the type of left-hander I have described or not. You should correct as soon as possible any weakness of yours I may have brought to light. However, not every right-hander knows how to exploit them. Take comfort, because the reverse situation usually applies. As a race, inexperienced right-handers dread playing left-handers.

12. MATCH PLAY

PLAY YOUR FIRST MATCH when you feel you are ready for it and are looking forward to gaining experience. Do not play from an anxious sense of duty or anything like that. Competing at the earliest possible moment, "sink or swim," may suit some individuals. For most players, however, this amounts to premature match play. They learn little or nothing from it, and become discouraged instead of being stimulated.

You are ready to play a match when you have a forehand you can attack with if the opportunity arises, a backhand that may not be good but at least feels strong, and a reliable second serve. You should also be able to lob, volley and smash (and perhaps half-volley as well) with a chance of success. Your attitude should be that you will try to win your first match, and if you don't, that you will learn from it.

There is not much point in playing a match any earlier or with a widely different attitude. If you cannot attack with *any* stroke, you cannot *win* your match. You will only be hoping or waiting for your opponent to lose it, and you will never learn to enjoy match play that way. You need the pleasant feeling of calling the tune, even if only sometimes. Nor do you want your backhand to feel weak, and you certainly do not want to look helpless when some other shot, such as a volley, comes along and you have no stroke for it. It only sets you back to face up to a match with a shaky second serve, and then serve a flock of double faults. As for attitude, if you are not alert to win and interested to learn, you may feel paralyzed at the start of the match and in a half-daze for the rest of it.

So much for anyone's first match. I will not load any more on your shoulders, or you may hardly remember to watch the ball. If you are ready for your first match, play it.

Your Later Matches

Let us now imagine that you have played several matches (as you may well have done already), but that all sorts of things are not clear to you. For instance, are you the only one who's nervous, and how many matches will you have to play before you're not nervous? How do you make a match feel like a practice set that you're used to? How do you *start* a match calmly? What is a clear example of tactics? And so on. Well then, here are a few facts in the world of match play.

Tension

People who say a match means no more to them than a social set does, are not really interested in their tennis. Whenever anyone is interested in a match he will feel some degree of tension. However, so will his opponent. You should know this, no matter how unconcerned your opponent may choose to appear.

Pre-match Nervousness

What you are nervous about before a match is your strokes. But you will not be starting with match-point against you, or at game-point, or even at any point. You will play your first strokes in the warm-up where they don't count. Remember that, and you will substantially reduce pre-match nervousness.

Match Nervousness

This is almost entirely due to wishing for the match to end

victoriously *while* you are in the midst of playing it. You need to put the final result out of your mind and play for one point at a time—in a rally, for one stroke at a time.

You will not be able to forget the final result entirely. No one can. However, with each match you play it will affect your strokes less, because each match teaches you again and again to concentrate on the stroke you are playing. Play the stroke as well as you can, not worrying about its result *while* you are playing it. Let action take over from worry.

Match Routine

Arrive in good time. Rather than becoming nervous waiting about, you are likely to be unsettled and perhaps even flustered if you are late and have to rush onto the court.

Decide, before you spin your racket for service, whether you want to serve or receive, or, should you lose the spin, which end you want to start from. If you keep ahead of things, you won't feel dazed or faintly unreal.

In the warm-up, go through your normal practice-set routine. Watch the ball, turn sideways, aim with long contact over the net and straight down the middle to your opponent, come to the net and feel your wrist get stronger with each volley, ask for a few lobs to loosen up your overhead, and go back to the baseline and serve about half a dozen serves from each side. Do not rely on being allowed practice serves after a set has started (and do not practice this way, if you have, any longer). Expect the warm-up to be short.

Starting

"Play" is called (or you and opponent decide to start) and you are to serve. It is utterly useless to wish that the match were over and you had won it. And it is equally useless to lash out with your first serve of the match for a desperation ace, to make you feel better. Instead: stand near the center mark; line

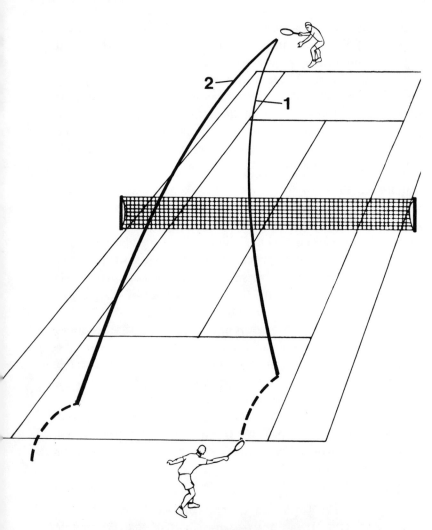

Illus. 36. **ATTACKING YOUR OPPONENT'S BACKHAND.** If you aim first to his backhand, he may step around it. Trying harder, you may hit into the alley. Drive first to his forehand, *then* to his backhand.

up the toes of your shoes; separate the balls; hold the first ball well forward between your finger ends and the ball of your thumb, and throw it well up; watch it settle; keep your back toe in contact with the ground; aim your serve with long contact, hit with the center of your strings and send the ball *over* the net. If a serve like that misses, it is at least a good sighter for your second. You will have taken your first step, responsibly.

Enjoy It

You should be clearly aware of enjoying matches and you should work toward this in each succeeding match. If you are enjoying the match you will have only your opponent to beat and not yourself as well. "Enjoyment" does not necessarily mean smiling pleasantly and feeling weak. There has always been such a thing as grim enjoyment. Choose any form you like, but choose one. You will play better match tennis that way. What is your alternative? Disliking the game?

Tactics

The most simple and effective case of tactics is to make every opportunity you can to play your strengths, and play your weaker strokes only when you cannot avoid them. If you can do this you will have the initiative, and the player having the initiative is always the winner.

If your forehand is a much better stroke than your backhand, run round the ball and play forehand after forehand. In trying to reach your backhand at all costs, your opponent may hit a lot of shots over your backhand sideline.

If your opponent plays these tactics against you (that is, if it is he who is playing a lot of forehands and covering his backhand) you should play first to his forehand side so that he must leave an open backhand court behind him—then drive into it. You can thus force him to play a backhand, instead of your being enticed to aim wider and wider to that side and unnecessarily hitting over the sideline. (See Illus. 36.)

If you are a left-hander with a strong forehand you should likewise make opportunities to use it. Try to entice your opponent into hitting over your backhand sideline. He may not know about hitting to your forehand first. If he does know and does hit there, then play your deep cross-court drive to his backhand corner. (See Illus. 35 again.)

Left-hander, move at once to your best position. This is a little to the right of the center mark, for two reasons. You want to cover your backhand, and the ball is on that side of the court anyway. If your cross-court shot is deep, your right-handed opponent will not easily reach your backhand, because not many players have a strong down-the-line backhand.

Now I must come to the assistance of a right-hander trying to oppose you. If a left-hander gives you this deep cross-court forehand and moves to his right behind his backline, and you feel he has his backhand covered, you should play a deep, diagonal cross-court backhand and await a better chance. If he has crowded too close to his backhand corner, a cross-court backhand from you that is short and wide may win the rally outright. Left-hander, if that cross-court backhand he just played is not very short and not very wide and you can reach it easily, you will have a shortish angled ball at the mercy of your forehand.

Not all right-handers are well balanced between forehand and backhand strength, nor do all left-handers have a forehand that is the best shot on the court. However, this is often the case.

A chapter, a book, could be written on tactics. Reading it before you gain practical experience from matches of your own would be overloading yourself with theory.

After the Match

If you win, do not leave the court without your opponent. If you lose, make no excuses whatsoever. Win or lose, practice again as soon as possible (on the same day if you can) because it is almost certain that some of your strokes did not feel sound. The best method of overcoming a weakness is to practice it, and the best time of all is immediately after a match. The moment the match ends you are mentally rested, and you do not need a physical rest. End your practice with a few shots from your best stroke. You should keep this weapon sharp, to cut with it as early as possible in your next match.

Post-graduate

You are now a match player, so my task is done. However, there is always something new and interesting ahead. Let's glance at one example, "anticipation," which is most appropriate at this point. Anticipating your opponent's actions adds yards to your speed about the court. It does not interfere with your watching the ball. At the same time as you are watching the ball, you will also see your opponent. If you doubt this, try not to see him. From the tell-tale way in which your opponent sets himself for his strokes he unwittingly sends you smoke signals. For example:

ONE. Your opponent wants to serve wide of your forehand in the right court. He may throw the ball more to his right, to help put a roundhouse curve on it. He may stand wider of the center mark than usual. He may even be one of the many players who use two different services—a sliced action to go to your forehand, and a topspin one to attack your backhand. Whichever of these types your opponent is, he warns you when he is about to serve wide to your forehand.

TWO. Another type of server may normally remain behind the backline, and follow his serve in every now and again to surprise you. There need be no surprise if his scuttle to the net is always preceded by a short quick throw and a hurried swing. He may as well have sent you a telegram.

THREE. Your opponent sends several forehand drives in similar fashion to your backhand. For his next forehand he sets himself differently, to meet the ball a little farther in front of him. From your end of the court you cannot possibly see the couple of inches involved in his meeting the ball earlier, but your opponent *looks* different. His cross-court drive to your forehand side is coming, possibly short and wide, with topspin. You can start to move just before he hits it.

FOUR. Players who do not aim their backhands with long contact often use two different backhand actions. For cross-court they pull the ball with topspin and for down-the-line they slice the racket against the inside surface of the ball. Their intended directions are obvious, and you can start to move as soon as you feel they are committed to one action and one direction.

FIVE. You come to the net, prepared for a passing shot to be attempted to either side of you. Just before hitting, your opponent seems to relax, and he takes his racket back low. He is going to lift the ball and try to lob over your head.

There are many more examples. Look for them in your opponents. You will not be disappointed. Even if you see your opponent's actions only subconsciously, it's enough. You're forewarned, and you feel yards or seconds quicker.

Won't an opponent then try to disguise his actions? He may succeed in disguising them sometimes, but only now and then. If a player forsakes the natural stroke-making he has built up and instead tries to do everything back to front, his whole game loses power and control. Try it and see.

Habits

You will also notice some habits of your opponents more and more as you continue to play matches. Here are some examples:

ONE. Many players, if you come to the net against their forehands, will try to drive past you, but if you advance against their backhands they will lob. This is particularly noticeable when both their shots have to be played on the run.

TWO. A certain opponent may always try to pass you across your body with topspin when the bounce is fairly high, and may always try to slide the ball down the line when it is low. Late in a close match your knowledge of this can be useful indeed.

THREE. Most players reaching forward to a backhand half-volley, normally play it cross-court. In a tight situation you can count on this.

Your Future

As you play more tennis and more matches you will learn more about the game yourself than this book has taught you. But don't part company with it forever. When your game lapses, look back at it. You'll find the reason. You'd just temporarily overlooked it. And then you're on your way once more.

INDEX